Quiet Water
NEW JERSEY

Canoe & Kayak Guide

2nd Edition

D0815651

Kathy Kenley

APPALACHIAN MOUNTAIN CLUB BOOKS
BOSTON, MASSACHUSETTS

To My Mother

Front cover photograph: Nancie Battaglia Photography
Back cover photographs (l-r): *Green Turtle Pond* © Kathy Kenley
                            Kayakers and *Canoeists* © David Brownell
Cover Design: Mac & Dent
Book Design: Amy Winchester
Map Design: Carol Bast Tyler & Katharine Donnelly
All interior photographs by the author unless otherwise noted.

Distributed by The Globe Pequot Press, Inc., Guilford, CT.

Library of Congress Cataloging-in-Publication data is available from
AMC Books. Call (617) 523-0636 ext. 328.

10 9 8 7 6 5 4 3 2 1   04   05   06   07   08

Contents

Acknowledgments vi
Introduction vii
How to Use This Book xxi
Map Legend xxiii
Trip Locator Map xxiv
Trip Highlights Chart xxvi

NORTHERN NEW JERSEY 1

  1. Steeny Kill and Sawmill Lakes 2

  2. Lake Aeroflex, Gardner's Pond,
     Twin Lakes, and Whites Pond 6

  3. Hackensack Meadows 10

  4. Pompton Lake 14

  5. Shepherd Lake 17

  6. Monksville Reservoir 20

  7. Green Turtle Pond 23

  8. Wawayanda Lake 26

  9. Swartswood and Paulins Kill Lakes 31

 10. White's Lake 36

 11. Oxford Furnace Lake 38

 12. Columbia Lake 40

 13. Merrill Creek Reservoir 42

 14. Lakes Hopatcong and Musconetcong 45

 15. Silver Lake 50

 16. Cranberry Lake 53

CENTRAL NEW JERSEY 57

17. Delaware and Raritan Canal 58

18. Lake Surprise 62

19. Lakes Carasaljo and Shenandoah 64

20. Manasquan Reservoir 69

21. Prospertown Lake 72

22. Assunpink, Stone Tavern, and Rising Sun Lakes 75

23. Forge Pond 78

24. Shadow Lake 80

25. Round Valley Reservoir 83

26. Spruce Run Reservoir 87

27. Lake Mercer 90

28. Lake Topanemus 92

29. Farrington Lake 94

30. Turn Mill Lake, Lake Success, and Colliers Mill Lake 98

31. Whitesbog Ponds 102

32. Weequahic Lake 105

SOUTHERN NEW JERSEY 109

33. Batsto Lake 110

34. Atsion Lake 116

35. Mannington Meadows 120

36. Stafford Forge Ponds 124

37. Newton Lake and Cooper River Park Lake 127

38. Shaw's Mill Pond 130

39. Manahawkin Impoundment and Bridge to Nowhere 132

40. East Creek Pond and Lake Nummy 138

41. Great Bay and the Edwin B. Forsythe National Wildlife Refuge . .141

42. Union Lake 145

43. Lake Oswego 149

44. Harrisville Pond 152

45. Wilson Lake 155

46. Lake Lenape 158

47. Lake Absegami 161

48. Corbin City Impoundments 164

49. Stewart Lake 168

50. Parvin Lake and Thundergust Lake 171

NATURE ESSAYS

Bowfin 30

Muskrat 55

Osprey 67

Pitcher Plant 96

Pine Barrens Tree Frog 119

Snowy Egret 136

Appendix: Resources 174
Alphabetical Listing of Lakes, Ponds, and Reservoirs 177
Leave No Trace 178
About the Author 179
About the AMC 180

Acknowledgments

First and foremost, I would like to thank the AMC for the opportunity to write this book and enjoy paddling many new sites in the process. My thanks go to Beth Krusi, editor, for her guidance and kind words along the way: her patience and understanding are appreciated.

Many people I met during this adventure helped me by supplying information about various sites and their surroundings. The list would be too long to singly name and thank all the park rangers, police officers, anglers, birders, and naturalists who gave their assistance. I met many local kayakers, canoeists, and anglers who extended their time and gave me information about their favorite places.

A special thanks to Professor Jack Connor of The Richard Stockton College of New Jersey, who not only helped review the introductory text material but gave me continual encouragement in writing about nature as well. My appreciation also goes to his colleague, Professor Mike Hozik, for his guidance in assembling the geologic history of the area and reviewing the final product.

I am deeply indebted to many friends: Karen Roseman, who spent countless hours drawing many of the site maps and helped with general research; Fran Orlofsky and Ted Ellis, who helped proofread site descriptions; and Mike Kelly, who helped with site investigations. I thank Bill Bell, of Bel Haven Canoe and Kayak, who provided valuable information on local wildlife. I extend appreciation to my kayaking friends who accompanied me on numerous trips and made them enjoyable, helping uncover information and giving encouragement throughout the project. This list includes Karen Roseman, Fran Orlofsky, Bill Bell, Linda Burdett, Gerard Marcus, Mike Kelly, Fred ("Fritz") Mitchel, and Mark Rogers.

Finally, warm love and appreciation go to my mother, who encouraged my interest in nature from an early age instead of making me play with dolls. Thanks, Mom.

Introduction

Most kids have a magnetic attraction to water, as evidenced by the number of puddles they'll go out of their way to jump in. Some of us never outgrow this attraction.

Something intangible, almost spiritual, happens when I place my boat on the water. Sitting quietly for a moment, I let the water's soothing bob realign my soul. I dip my paddle over the side and the little splash starts my transport on a magic liquid carpet ride. I watch an osprey hunt for fish or listen to the symphony of avian songs that makes me feel one with nature.

Other than some canoe experiences I had as a child in the Pocono Mountains of Pennsylvania, my paddling adventures began in my late teens when I stumbled across an old, small kayak at a garage sale. It was light enough to load and unload myself and, more importantly, it fit on the roof of my small car without extending past the bumpers—well, at least not too far. A strange sense of freedom came with that first boat, a freedom rimmed with both the excitement of adventure and the peacefulness of solitude. Opening local county maps, my eyes zoomed in on every splotch of blue; the search was on for the magic blue liquid.

Among my favorite places are quiet lakes, marshes, ponds, and slow-moving streams, where I can sit on the water and drink in the scenery and wildlife with all my senses. Seeing what animals live in this little cove or what might be found around the back of that island tweaks my curiosity. With each new site, I discover different habitats and learn the links between ecosystems—their similarities and their differences. As a naturalist, my binoculars, camera, field guides, and a journal usually accompany me.

One tactic I occasionally employ is to combine biking and paddling. I lock my bike to a tree on the downstream take-out of a waterway or the opposite end of the lake, then go to the put-in and start paddling. At the end of the trip, I lock up the boat, bike back to my vehicle, and drive back to pick up the boat. The bike rides range from fifteen to forty minutes, and it's a great way to see an area's land and water views and get an upper- and lower-body workout on the same outing. A few such trips are included in this book, although it is not necessary to take a bike along to enjoy these waters.

Why Quiet Waters?

When the opportunity to prepare this book for the Appalachian Mountain Club (AMC) arose, I gladly accepted it, to seek out new sites and visit those I hadn't paddled in years. Available books covered the many rivers that dissect the state, but none mentioned the hundreds of lakes, ponds, and reservoirs accessible to paddlers. Open skies over large bodies of water draw a different variety of wildlife, like ospreys, eagles, ducks, and certain hawks, which do not frequent narrow streams or rivers. These quiet waters offer their own special ambience, one suited to those who enjoy the tranquility of nature or want a respite, however brief, from hectic city life.

Livery services are necessary for trips down a river and are not conducive to picking up and paddling whenever you please, particularly if you prefer going solo. The serenity of lazily paddling in the middle of a lake, watching and listening to wildlife, is lost if you're being swept downstream by a current. During summer months, local rivers overflow with kayaks, canoes, and tubes, more reminiscent of an amusement park bumper-car ride than a pristine river. But on New Jersey lakes—even the busier ones on hot weekends—it isn't too difficult to find a peaceful area to enjoy. Quiet waters also are ideal for families taking children out for the first time, when a trip may need to end earlier than planned. Novices can gain experience in the calm and unthreatening environment of lakes and ponds. As an experienced paddler, I visit a small local pond a few times each spring just to check out my equipment and practice different strokes and maneuvers before venturing out on longer paddles.

The Selection Process

What's the recipe for a book such as this? Take a couple of weeks' poring over detailed county and topographic maps, thousands of road miles, a few hundred water miles, fifteen-plus rolls of film, a dozen small notepads, lots of camp food, and mix well. My culinary skills did not improve, but my repertoire of paddling sites escalated tenfold. Along the way I learned how to put my mini van into "squeeze gear" on narrow roads and teased it into becoming four-wheel drive for short distances. We have some absolutely delightful gems within our state that I encourage all who read this book to visit. If you don't, you'll be missing some of the best paddling adventures in the Northeast. Of the more than 140 sites that I investigated, I selected 50 locations (69 lakes and ponds) for inclusion.

How did I make my final choices for this book? My main focus was to provide information on the better sites available throughout the state to assist those just getting started and increase the repertoire of more experienced paddlers. After consulting with my regular paddling buddies, I also made it a goal to have a wide enough geographic selection of sites to provide a location within forty-five minutes of anyone, from the beginner who wishes to get out frequently for experience, to parents initiating their children into the sport, to someone who simply cannot travel longer distances. Toward that end, a few sites have been included that may seem less than ideal for the more experienced paddler out for a full day on wilderness waters.

Obviously, some counties have an abundance of lakes. In a few counties I could have spent a solid month investigating every body of water larger than 20 acres, but this book would never have been finished. Where lake density was thick, I tried to choose the best body of water, not necessarily the biggest or the most popular. Other counties exhibited a paucity of selection due to lack of topography or inaccessibility. I kept a record of every site visited, including those rejected (along with the reason for their exclusion). Try as I might, I didn't quite attain my personal goal of a site within forty-five minutes of anyone, but I came close.

If you're out for the quietest paddling, select sites offering only boating, fishing, and possibly camping; swimming, picnicking, and recreational facilities tend to draw large crowds, particularly in July and August. If the whole family is out for the day, and you are the only one who paddles, you will want sites that provide additional recreational activities for the family to enjoy. What each of us looks for on any given day is different—some days it's a long, silent paddle; other days we just need something big enough to float our boat. The trip highlights chart will help guide you to the sites that meet your needs.

Equipment

Any book on paddling must have sections on equipment, technique, and safety. For those of you who are experienced paddlers, please take a moment to review these sections. For those just starting to paddle, I offer only preliminary tips and advice, because numerous books detail equipment, paddling techniques, and boat styles far better than I can in an abbreviated format. (See the appendix, Resources, for a list of some good ones.)

Four necessary pieces of equipment are: a canoe or kayak, an appropriate paddle, a first-aid kit, and a personal flotation device (PFD). I would add to that a whistle and a hand bilge pump or large boat sponge.

If you're old enough, you remember a time when there were only two types of sneakers: Converse high-tops or regular. Today sneaker designs exist for every sport and then some. The same is true for kayaks and canoes to some degree. There are styles for whitewater, rodeo, sea, surf, touring, and racing—enough to set even the more experienced paddler's head spinning. Don't let the endless styles overwhelm you. Since your main interest is paddling quiet waters, you'll want a boat that is stable and tracks well. If you intend to camp or carry extensive camera equipment, make sure the volume of the boat is large enough to carry the desired gear. Your best bet is to rent a boat a few times until you get the feel of paddling and are comfortable. Outfitters gladly recommend models they feel will best suit your needs and your physical characteristics such as height and weight. When you're ready to buy, find a boat that handles well for your current skill level—you can always upgrade later.

Dealers located near a lake usually let you test-paddle different models for little or no fee. Paddle fests held late spring through early fall offer a great opportunity to try out a number of boats. Some rental operations offer end-of-season sales on used boats—a great way to pick up a boat inexpensively. Most of all, make sure you're comfortable in the boat.

Materials also vary. Roto-molded plastic is the least expensive and best for beginners, because it can stand up to quite a bit of abuse. Fiberglass increases the cost tremendously and, although the boat will move faster than its plastic counterpart, is more susceptible to damage from rocks or gravelly bottoms. Plastic and fiberglass models are comparable in weight and occupy the heavier side of the spectrum. Kevlar increases the cost but decreases weight substantially. Carbon fiber is the lightest and most expensive but is more susceptible to damage.

Camera and binoculars add to the enjoyment of wildlife observation, but they should be kept in waterproof bags—also referred to as dry bags—until ready for use. Dry bags come in a variety of sizes suitable for anything from a small camera to a tent. I keep a small dry bag in the cockpit of my kayak for items frequently used such as sunscreen, sunglasses, camera, guidebooks, and binoculars. Another dry bag behind the seat carries extra clothes in case the day turns chilly or wet.

Always take plenty of water if you intend to be on the water for any length of time. The heat of a summer's day or the dry west winds of fall can bring on dehydration. And how about a small journal? It can serve as not only a log of sites paddled but also a reference for wildlife observations and friends you've paddled with or met along the way. A change of clothes and a towel kept in your boat are handy just in case you get caught in a rainstorm or have an otherwise soggy trip.

If you plan to visit sites where you have to carry your boat any distance, wheeled carts and canoe yokes are available. The carts are compact and fold up to store neatly in the bottom of your boat. Wash all your gear with clean, fresh water at the end of a trip and dry thoroughly to prevent corrosion and mold.

Technique

Unlike whitewater or ocean paddling, quiet water requires no special skills, but knowing how to hold a paddle correctly and properly execute the basic forward, backward, sideways (draw), and turning strokes will make for a more enjoyable day. It's always better to learn correct technique initially than to correct sloppy habits later.

If you can, find the time to take a quick lesson. Most outfitters offer private and group instruction for beginning and experienced paddlers. A half-hour to one-hour lesson is all you need to start off in the right direction. Novices should stay with smaller ponds before tackling large lakes, where wind and waves could challenge them beyond their capabilities. Most lakes are glasslike in the early-morning hours, but as an old salt once told me, "As the sun comes up, so does the wind." This adage holds true for both the ocean and the lake down the street.

For those of you who have some experience, continue to refine current skills and add new ones. Braces and self-rescue techniques should be learned prior to venturing out to the middle of a large lake or reservoir. Take a few minutes to review these skills at the beginning and periodically throughout your paddling season. You may never need them, but if a squall arises suddenly or a large boat passes dangerously close, you will be prepared. Increasing your skill level will not only make you feel more comfortable with your boat, but also instill a level of confidence in case less-than-ideal conditions arise—and they eventually will.

Basic navigation skills come in handy on larger lakes, where rainstorms or fog can obscure the shoreline suddenly. (Most prevalent in early morning and late afternoon during spring and fall, fog is due to a marked difference between land and air temperatures.) Always bring a compass and know how to use it properly.

Safety

The single most important piece of safety equipment is the personal flotation device (PFD), also called a life jacket or life vest, with a waterproof whistle attached. The PFD should always be worn, because even the most experienced paddlers can find themselves on the wrong side of the waterline. Some lakes and reservoirs require that you wear a PFD at all times or have one readily accessible within thirty seconds. Don the vest immediately if fog, inclement weather, or other hazardous conditions arise. Nonswimmers and children should always wear a PFD, with straps secured tightly enough to prevent the vest from slipping off. Children should not wear an adult PFD, because they can easily slip out of it; make sure they have a child's vest with a crotch strap that fits properly.

Unless you have a propensity for a particular color or feel you must make a fashion statement, select a yellow or orange PFD, particularly for children or nonswimmers. Light colors are seen more readily against a dark water surface, facilitating quicker rescue. PFDs also add a bit of warmth on chilly days. Small children riding in a canoe or in the front compartment of a tandem (two-person) kayak should be warned not to lean over the side, stand up, or move about suddenly.

Motorboats of more than 10 horsepower are loud and can be unsettling to novice paddlers when they zip by, throwing large wakes. If caught unexpectedly, turn the bow of your boat into the wake as quickly as possible to prevent swamping. Most waters listed in this book either do not permit motors or impose a maximum size of 10 horsepower. Fortunately, many lakes ban personal watercraft altogether, and more than one lake bans their use on weekends during summer. Wildlife management areas, except for Union and Prospertown Lakes, prohibit gasoline motors. In addition, many bodies of water are located within or adjacent to prime hunting areas. Check with your local state fish and game official or local sporting goods store for specific hunting seasons, particularly in spring and fall.

Water robs the body of heat twenty-five times faster than air, potentially causing a condition called hypothermia, or subnormal body temperature. Drowning may occur when extended immersion in cold water cools the body to such a degree that a person becomes physically and mentally incapacitated. Symptoms of hypothermia include slurred speech, loss of coordination, confusion, apathy, and irrational behavior; all symptoms become more critical when you are paddling solo. Prime conditions for hypothermia exist in spring and early summer, when water temperatures are cold but warm air lulls us into wearing less-than-adequate clothing for coldwater immersion. Roll up your long-sleeved shirt if you must, but don't take it off. Should you accidentally upset your boat, put your PFD on immediately and roll down those sleeves. A PFD not only adds a small amount of insulation, but will also keep you afloat should you lose consciousness. Change into warm, dry clothes as soon as practical and drink warm liquids. Pick up a pamphlet on hypothermia from your local hospital or American Red Cross chapter to learn more.

If you paddle solo, let someone know where you are going, especially if you live alone. In big-boat arenas, it's called a float plan. Recently, a very experienced friend who lives alone went kayaking down a local river swollen with rains. He hit a submerged log, quickly found himself inspecting the river bottom, and surfaced with his head just inches from a fat overhanging tree limb. "I could have been knocked unconscious and nobody would have known where I was!" he said. "And the water was cold—I could have gone hypothermic." We discussed the incident among our circle of paddling friends, promising to send an e-mail or call someone whenever we go out alone, and let them know when we return.

Taking the Children Along

Paddling with children is rewarding but requires special considerations. In addition to wearing a PFD, impress on them the importance of proper movement while in a boat, such as moving slowly without sudden moves, sitting and staying low in the boat, and knowing the proper procedure for entering and exiting the boat. Plan on shorter trips initially. Long paddles may require you to land occasionally and let the kids romp around a bit, even if the space is small, depending on their normal activity level. Most children are so excited to be going out in a boat that they sit quietly and absorb the sights and sounds—at least the first few times out.

Try to include them in the adventure. Play games that involve spotting specific turtles or birds. Ask their opinion on which way to go, or what they think about the scenery in a particular cove. Inexpensive binoculars or a disposable camera will help engage them in nature observations. Having some equipment to call their own, and being responsible for it, will help make them feel part of the trip. Very young children may want to bring along a special toy, perhaps a small one that won't get ruined if it gets wet.

Kids eat—often! Be sure to pack enough snacks and drinks for the paddle as well as for the trip home. Pack an extra sweater or jacket for them, even in summer, because a light breeze over cool mountain waters or in dense shade near shore can be chilly for those not paddling. A change of clothes kept in the car will be handy if they accidentally trip and fall into the water getting in or out of the boat.

Something happens when they get between eight and ten years old—they want to paddle; not just hold a paddle, but be part of the actual process. Child-sized canoe and kayak paddles are available, and if you want to keep the peace and avert mutiny, buy one. Keeping kids in a tandem kayak while they're learning techniques only works for a short time. Once they get the hang of it, they'll want their own kayak. In canoes, you'll be able to stretch this out a little longer by teaching them both bow and stern techniques before they can adequately handle their own boat. Enjoy the experience of sharing this wonderful world with children.

Wildlife

It's a well-known maxim among wildlife photographers, birders, and other serious nature observers that once you are in an area of abundant wildlife, sit still. Let them come to you, and you have a better chance of closer observation for longer periods of time. Dawn and dusk are the best times to spot deer, raccoons, otter, and other mammals that come to drink water. Look for animal tracks near tiny openings around the lakes they frequent, get into position ahead of time, and then wait quietly and patiently for their arrival.

Do not feed wildlife, and never attempt to touch or approach wild animals. Raccoons, bears, skunks, foxes, and coyotes are potential visitors to your campsite and may be encountered while hiking, particularly in the mountainous northern regions. Raccoons and bears have been known to open coolers and rummage through food containers; keep food tightly packed and stored in your vehicle or away from the campsite—never in your tent. Clean all cooking implements immediately after use, and place garbage where animals cannot smell it or gain access to it.

Any wild animal can harbor diseases such as rabies. Never approach or chase after an animal; you can disrupt its daily routine and frighten it into defending itself or its territory. In addition, never get between a wild animal and its young. If you accidentally find yourself in this situation, lower your eyes and back away slowly. Should you be bitten or scratched accidentally, seek medical attention immediately.

Jersey, along with other Mid-Atlantic and New England states, is home to *Ixodes scapularis*, the deer tick that carries the bacteria responsible for Lyme disease. This tick normally crawls around on the body for three or more hours before settling on a spot. It takes another hour or two before burrowing deep into the skin. While you do have plenty of time before a tick can do damage, it is wise to check yourself often if you brush past foliage while loading or unloading your boat. Always make a thorough check for ticks at the end of the day.

Tick kits, available at most outdoor and sporting goods stores, contain a small magnifying glass, specialized tweezers, and instructions on proper removal, as well as common signs and symptoms of Lyme disease. A bull's-eye rash, the most obvious sign, often develops within a day or two around the bite, but not everyone is lucky enough to develop this symptom. Lyme disease is easily treated if detected early.

Fishing, Crabbing, and Permits

Catching your own dinner, whether camping overnight or returning home, is a rewarding experience. If you are camping, bring along some add-water-and-heat meals—just in case the fish are not biting that day. Break-apart rods that come in two or three sections are relatively inexpensive and stow compactly in even the smallest boat. Rod holders are available for canoes and kayaks.

Blue crabs, at their peak in August, can be caught in brackish coastal regions from late June through September. Crabbing requires no license, but current state law requires a legal minimum size of 4.5 inches across the body, tip to tip.

Be advised that anyone between the ages of sixteen and sixty-nine must have and display a valid New Jersey fishing license to fish New Jersey's fresh waters. Licenses can be obtained from most county or municipal offices or agents, such as sporting goods stores and bait shops. Year-round resident and nonresident licenses are available, as are two- and seven-day licenses. Special licenses are available for senior residents (age sixty-five and older). To obtain a resident license, you must have lived in New Jersey for six months immediately prior to the time of application. If you are a New Jersey resident seventy years of age or older, no fishing license is required, but you must carry acceptable proof of age, such as a driver's license.

Geography

Although New Jersey is small, its geography and geology provide a diversity of ecosystems within relatively short distances of each other. Crystal-clear mountain lakes, salt- and freshwater marshes, sweet cedar swamps, and hardwood forests each offer their own special scenery and wildlife.

New Jersey is a peninsula, attached to the North American continent by a 50-mile-wide strip along its northern border, shared with New York. It is bounded on the far northeast by the Hudson River, on the east by the Atlantic Ocean, on the west by the Delaware River, and on the south-southwest by brackish Delaware Bay. Along the Atlantic coast, numerous barrier islands offer protection from storm waves for populated towns on the mainland. Temperatures vary slightly between the northern and southern parts of the state, with the southern coastal region being the warmest. In winter the ameliorating effect of the Atlantic Ocean along the coast contrasts with the chilly heights of the northern mountains. During much of the summer, ocean breezes help cool coastal regions.

If you mention the Appalachian Mountains, chances are that most people will imagine the mountainous states of Virginia, West Virginia, and Pennsylvania; yet the Appalachian Ridge and Valley Region can be seen in the northwest corner of New Jersey. A flat coastal plain that some may find mundane comprises more than half the state's land. Go to a brackish pond or back bay where various shorebirds can be seen, then visit the rusty, tannin-stained waters of a cedar swamp and you'll find two very different environments.

A Brief Lesson in Geology

The earth is a living planet, undergoing daily change. Its outer surface, or crust, is broken up into plates, which move about the surface at seemingly imperceptible rates of 4 centimeters per year on average. These minuscule year-to-year movements over millions and millions of years have produced large changes in the landscape.

Plates basically do three things: collide, break apart, or slide past each other. When plates collide, some of the land between is crumpled and uplifted, creating mountain ranges such as the Appalachian and Sierra Nevada.

A different process occurs when a large plate or landmass breaks apart, creating two smaller plates. This is going on today in East Africa in an area called the Great Rift Valley, which possesses the greatest rupture on the earth's land surface and is one of the few features visible from space. Given another ten million years or so, Africa's landmass will probably occupy two separate plates.

When plates slide past one another and the tension that has built up along that boundary is suddenly released, earthquakes occur. The example most Americans are familiar with is the San Andreas Fault, where the Pacific plate is sliding past the North American plate as it has done for millions of years. Some readers probably remember the 1989 Loma Prieta earthquake that occurred during the World Series in Oakland, California, a city situated along the San Andreas Fault.

About 550 million years ago, a huge landmass began to rift in a jagged pattern, which would eventually form the edges of the present-day African and North American plates. A few crumbs broke off during rifting, leaving behind smaller landmasses. Volcanic ridges formed as the crust thinned over a long period of time. Before the rifting was complete, the two large parts of the original landmass began moving back toward each other. One of the small landmasses in between, called the Piedmont, was thrust onto the margin of the North American side, resulting in the formation of the ancestral Appalachian Mountains around 500 million years ago. As those mountains eroded, rain and wind carried small particles south and southeast toward the sea, creating the base of a low-lying coastal plain. During this time, Africa was still moving closer to North America.

During the next 300 million years, global events allowed the sea to advance and retreat several times over the lower elevations, each time leaving behind saltwater sediments along with some of the animals that inhabited those shallow seas. Finally, around 250 million years ago, Africa collided with North America, compressing, folding, and uplifting the lands in between in a mountain-building event that created the present-day Appalachians. While the Appalachians extend from Newfoundland to South Carolina, the brunt of the impact took place between New York and southern Maryland, creating a series of wrinkles in the land roughly parallel to our continental edge. Today we refer to this prominent system of land features as the Appalachian Ridge and Valley Region. Folded layers of rocks are visible in many roadcuts throughout the northern part of the state. (Do not examine them while driving!) Shallow ocean sediments also were lifted onto the land, and today fossil-hunting enthusiasts find remnants of these ancient seas from Bound Brook in central New Jersey to High Point in the extreme northwest corner.

About 200 million years ago, Africa and North America began to separate again and, as rifting progressed, volcanic activity started that would eventually form the Watchung and Orange Mountains and the Palisades Sill. This volcanic activity lasted 500,000 years, but the breakup wasn't complete until about 180 million years ago. Bit by bit the new mountains started eroding; wind and rain carried sediments eastward in a process that continues today.

Within the past few hundred thousand years, in a period known as the Wisconsin Ice Age, ice sheets advanced and retreated several times over North America, occasionally reaching as far south as Trenton. Though the last ice age ended 10,000 to 12,000 years ago, it left its mark on the terrain. Each time the ice advanced, glaciers carved broad valleys, scoured and gouged the land, and ground down the mountains. When the climate warmed and the glaciers retreated, meltwater washed particles of sand and gravel previously locked within the ice sheet to the south and southeast. Today hundreds of feet of this sand and gravel form the top layers of land in the southern half of New Jersey. Occasionally glaciers would pick up large chunks of rock and transport them within the ice sheet. After the ice melted, these rocks, called erratics, were left behind, often tens of miles from their original sources.

With the exception of recent glacial and volcanic activities, humans were not around during the events that shaped the earth's landforms. Today geologists examine the workings of present-day processes and combine this knowledge with evidence from rocks to develop theories about when a geologic process happened.

What to Expect in New Jersey

New Jersey lies in the highly populated Northeast Corridor between two major cities: Philadelphia and New York City. Let's not kid ourselves. We cannot expect to find within our borders as many remote areas per square mile as in (say) Maine or Montana, but we do have many beautiful bodies of water to paddle, some quite isolated. I have found many lakes in more "remote" regions to be extremely crowded and unappealing—houses line the shores down to the water's edge, while motorboats and personal watercraft roil the waters like a storm. Other places are rimmed with private property, or are posted for "township residents only," depriving the public of access. In contrast, some lakes and ponds within highly populated towns proved a very lovely surprise, with dense woods surrounding some or all of the shore and private houses set well back from the banks. A few of these lakes had only a narrow, landscaped swath surrounding them, sometimes with meandering biking and walking trails, but they were still pleasant oases in the midst of a large urban setting.

We don't have bumper stickers from New Jersey that read, "This car climbed Mount So-And-So." What mountains we do have in the northwestern quadrant of the state are small, with 1,804-foot High Point Mountain in High Point State Park being the greatest elevation in the state. Yet within these mountains are some absolutely delightful pristine lakes beset with islands and interesting coves.

In the flat coastal plain of southern New Jersey, Apple Pie Hill rises meekly to a whopping 183 feet above sea level. If it weren't for the damming of rivers in this region, I doubt there would be any lakes deep enough to paddle. In reality, most New Jersey lakes and ponds have been dammed to some degree, increasing their holding capacity and acreage for recreational use or irrigation. Reservoirs, of course, are waterways dammed expressly for use in times of drought, even though they may have been large lakes initially.

Since more than half the state is a low-lying coastal plain bordering the Atlantic Ocean and Delaware Bay, you'll find a number of sites in tidal saltwater and brackish marshes carefully chosen for their minimal current. Although first-timers have paddled these waters with no problem, I strongly advise gaining some experience on other waters first. It is equally important to know tide schedules. Starting your trip against the current while you are still fresh and letting it help you on the way back is best. Make your first trips short, until you get the feel of tidal currents for that particular waterway. These habitats contain extensive wildlife, making it well worth the effort.

You and the Environment

The more often you get out to enjoy the ponds and lakes of New Jersey, the more you will appreciate our precious ecosystems and understand the need to help protect them. Numerous community organizations, college clubs, and paddling clubs host cleanups of various waterways. They are usually well advertised, and paddlers can join in the effort. Perhaps in the future you could organize an annual cleanup of your favorite location. On an individual level, my friends and I often carry a trash bag with us to remove carelessly discarded refuse. It may be a small effort, but it makes the waters cleaner for everyone and safer for wildlife. It's a good idea to carry a trash bag or two in your vehicle anyway, because many sites lack refuse containers, having a "carry-in, carry-out" policy instead. Books such as *Soft Paths* offer a wide variety of tips for hikers and campers to minimize their impact, helping to protect and preserve our environment. For more information on minimizing your impact on our natural resources, contact Leave No Trace at 800-332-4100 or www.LNT.org (see page 180).

The New Jersey Audubon Society acquires and maintains wildlife sanctuaries that protect wildlife and natural habitats, and educational centers that foster environmental awareness. The society currently maintains seven major sanctuaries and is responsible in part for twenty-two others. Many of its on-premises programs and community-sponsored events are perfect for the younger generation. The Nature Conservancy places its emphasis on the identification and preservation of ecologically important areas and endangered species. Look to the Sierra Club for involvement with environmental concerns and to join organized hikes sponsored around the state.

The Appalachian Mountain Club fosters public awareness of environmental and conservation issues through its books, publications, and workshops while promoting enjoyment of outdoor recreational activities with minimal impact. With protection of our ecosystems at the forefront, the AMC has spearheaded numerous conservation programs and has helped cofound several organizations. The AMC Mohican Outdoor Center, located in the 70,000-acre Delaware Water Gap National Recreation Area, is a great base for outdoor exploration in New Jersey. Check out the AMC website, www.outdoors.org, for more information.

The New York–New Jersey Trail Conference, based in Manhattan, maintains more than 1,000 miles of trails in two states, and monitors 7,600 acres of National Park Service lands that are part of the Appalachian Trail system. Its water-resistant trail maps are conveniently sized for backpacking or paddling. The goal of the New Jersey Division of Fish and Wildlife is to protect habitats necessary to maintain species diversity and wildlife distribution, while at the same time balancing commercial and recreational interests.

What a thrill it is to see tax dollars and voter opinions at work through the state-sponsored Green Acres Program, which provides loans and grants to various governmental agencies and nonprofit organizations in order to purchase properties and develop them into parks. The list is too long to enumerate every site at which parklands are due completely or in part to this program. To date the Green Acres Program has helped preserve almost half a million acres, and the numbers keep climbing.

You should keep abreast of any purchases of land around lakes by such agencies as Green Acres, The Nature Conservancy, the New Jersey Division of Fish and Wildlife, and others that open up lakes to public access. Pay attention to election issues like bond referendums allocating funds to acquire lands for preservation. Whatever we can do to help protect and preserve our environment also will ensure that we have scenic waters to paddle and wildlife to observe. (See the appendix for more information about the organizations mentioned above.)

How to Use This Book

Each of this book's paddles includes a description of the lake and surrounding area, directions for getting there, a basic map showing roads and launch areas, and information on what you can expect to see. Campgrounds come and campgrounds go; for this reason, I've focused on listing those lying within the premises of the lake property. For up-to-date information, it is best to purchase a campground guide; suggested books are listed in the appendix.

Maps and directions in this book are for near-site use only. Complement a large state map with county maps for finer detail, which becomes important in urban areas. County maps are also handy in backcountry areas, where route signs may not be displayed at reasonable intervals or properly indicated at critical junctions. Unless otherwise noted, parking for all sites is within 100 feet of the launch.

To further confuse matters, backcountry roads also have a habit of changing names at every little hamlet and junction. A topographic map book, such as those produced by DeLorme and others, will show not only topographic features but also many unimproved roads not indicated on county maps. Topographic maps of individual quadrangles are the best for exploring remote areas. They show almost all unimproved roads and trails, one of which may provide the only access to a new pond (for map sources, see the appendix).

Various state parks, particularly those with recreational facilities, charge an entrance fee from Memorial Day through Labor Day. A few of these have a separate fee to access the boat ramp. For an additional fee, you can buy a permit from any state park office that allows unlimited access to most state parks. With the exception of Union Lake, only electric outboards are allowed on wildlife management area waters in New Jersey.

While scouting for potential sites, I talked to people—park rangers, paddlers, local police officers, anglers, guides, and anyone I thought might know what was going on in the area. The outcome was information on a site scheduled to open for public access: Whites Pond in Sussex County. I also found one site that had recently opened up,

Paulins Kill Lake in Sussex County and another that is now closed, preventing me from making a long trip for nothing or, worse yet, confronting an irate landowner.

This book can never be complete. Lands around lakes and ponds are bought and sold continually, voiding or allowing public access. New housing developments and roads that spring up may render a site much less desirable or accessible. With your help, future editions of this book can include additional paddling sites and updated information on current ones. Your opinions and thoughts about these sites are important. Perhaps you know of a good lake I missed, notice some inaccuracy in this edition, or discover changes to existing sites. If so, please pass them along to me: Kathy Kenley, c/o AMC Books, 5 Joy Street, Boston, MA 02108. Enjoy the adventure—now, get out and paddle!

Map Legend

▬▬▬▬▬▬	Major highway
─────────	Highway or road
┅┅┅┅┅┅	Dirt road
┄ ┄ ┄ ┄ ┄	Footpath
┼┼┼┼┼┼┼	Railroad track
∿→	Stream (arrow indicates direction of flow)
▪▬▬▬▬▪	Dike
P	Parking area
⌣	Boat access
⋏	Marsh
⌂	Tents
◢	Lean-to
⌂	Cabin
⊓	Picnic area
⌐	Playground
☼	Hill
▭	Old foundation/ruin
■	Park headquarters/visitor's center

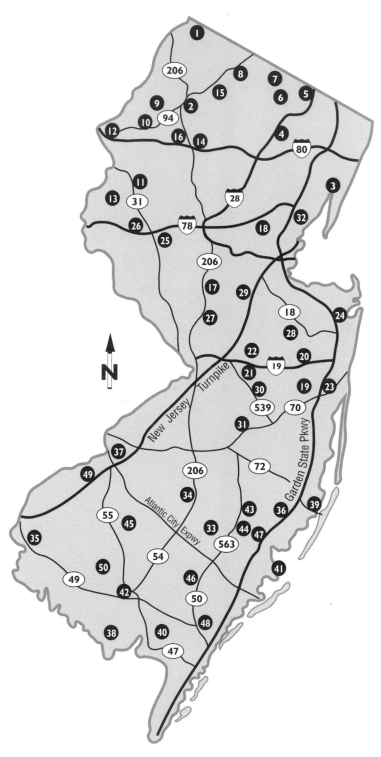

New Jersey

Trip Locator Map

1. Steeny Kill and Sawmill Lakes
2. Lake Aeroflex, Gardner's Pond, Twin Lakes, and Whites Pond
3. Hackensack Meadows
4. Pompton Lake
5. Shepherd Lake
6. Monksville Reservoir
7. Green Turtle Pond
8. Wawayanda Lake
9. Swartswood and Paulins Kill Lakes
10. White's Lake
11. Oxford Furnace Lake
12. Columbia Lake
13. Merrill Creek Reservoir
14. Lakes Hopatcong and Musconetcong
15. Silver Lake
16. Cranberry Lake
17. Delaware and Raritan Canal
18. Lake Surprise
19. Lakes Carasaljo and Shenandoah
20. Manasquan Reservoir
21. Prospertown Lake
22. Assunpink, Stone Tavern, and Rising Sun Lakes
23. Forge Pond
24. Shadow Lake
25. Round Valley Reservoir
26. Spruce Run Reservoir
27. Lake Mercer
28. Lake Topanemus
29. Farrington Lake
30. Turn Mill Lake, Lake Success, and Colliers Mill Lake
31. Whitesbog Ponds
32. Weequahic Lake
33. Batsto Lake
34. Atsion Lake
35. Mannington Meadows
36. Stafford Forge Ponds
37. Newton Lake and Cooper River Park Lake
38. Shaw's Mill Pond
39. Manahawkin Impoundment and Bridge to Nowhere
40. East Creek Pond and Lake Nummy
41. Great Bay and the Edwin B. Forsythe National Wildlife Refuge
42. Union Lake
43. Lake Oswego
44. Harrisville Pond
45. Wilson Lake
46. Lake Lenape
47. Lake Absegami
48. Corbin City Impoundments
49. Stewart Lake
50. Parvin Lake and Thundergust Lake

Trip Highlights Chart

TRIP	PAGE NO.	AREA/LENGTH	CAMPING	HIKING	MOTORS PERMITTED
Northern New Jersey					
1. Steeny Kill and Sawmill Lakes	2	50 acres	yes	no	yes
2. Lake Aeroflex, Gardner's Pond, Twin Lakes and Whites Pond	5	160 acres	yes	yes	yes
3. Hackensack Meadows	9	5 miles	yes	yes	no
4. Pompton Lake	12	204 acres	yes	yes	no
5. Shepherd Lake	15	74 acres	yes	no	yes
6. Monksville Reservoir	18	505 acres	no	yes	no
7. Green Turtle Pond	21	40 acres	no	no	yes
8. Wawayanda Lake	25	255 acres	no	yes	yes
9. Swartswood and Paulins Kill Lakes	28	744 acres	no	yes	yes
10. White's Lake	31	70 acres	no	yes	no
11. Oxford Furnace Lake	35	53 acres	yes	no	no
12. Columbia Lake	38	55 acres	yes	no	yes
13. Merrill Creek Reservoir	42	650 acres	yes	no	no
14. Lakes Hopatcong and Musconetcong	45	2685 and 329 acres	yes	no	yes
15. Silver Lake	48	21 acres	no	yes	yes
16. Cranberry Lake	51	179 acres/4 miles	yes	yes	yes
Central New Jersey					
17. Delaware and Raritan Canal	55	15 miles	yes	yes	yes

TRIP	PAGE NO.	AREA/LENGTH	CAMPING	HIKING	MOTORS PERMITTED
18. Lake Surprise	58	25 acres	yes	yes	yes/no
19. Lakes Carasaljo and Shenandoah	61	117 acres	yes	yes	no
20. Manasquan Reservoir	65	720 acres	no	yes	yes
21. Prospertown Lake	69	80 acres	no	yes	yes
22. Assunpink, Stone Tavern, and Rising Sun Lakes	71	315 acres	no	yes	yes
23. Forge Pond	74	45 acres	no	yes	yes
24. Shadow Lake	77	88 acres	no	yes	yes
25. Round Valley Reservoir	80	2350 acres/5 miles	yes	no	yes
26. Spruce Run Reservoir	85	1290 acres/3 miles	yes	no	no
27. Lake Mercer	88	275 miles	yes	no	no
28. Lake Topanemus	91	21 acres	no	no	no
29. Farrington Lake	94	290 acres	yes	yes	no
30. Turn Mill Lake, Lake Success, and Colliers Mill Lake	97	157 acres	yes	no	yes
31. Whitesbog Ponds	99	39 acres	yes	yes	no
32. Weequahic Lake,	102	80 acres	yes	yes	yes
Southern New Jersey					
33. Batsto Lake	107	40 acres	yes	no	no
34. Atsion Lake	110	62 acres/7.5/3 miles	yes	no	no

TRIP	PAGE NO.	AREA/LENGTH	CAMPING	HIKING	MOTORS PERMITTED
35. Mannington Meadows	113	2000+ acres/3 miles	yes	yes	yes
36. Stafford Forge Ponds	116	148 acres	yes	no	no
37. Newton Lake and Cooper River Park Lake	122	190 acres	no	no	yes
38. Shaw's Mill Pond	127	30 acres	yes	no	yes/no
39. Manahawkin Impoundment and Bridge to Nowhere	131	35 acres/3+ miles	no	no	no/yes
40. East Creek Pond and Lake Nummy	134	88 acres	yes	no	yes
41. Great Bay (Edwin B. Forsythe National Wildlife Refuge)	138	44 acres	yes	yes	no
42. Union Lake	140	898 acres	yes	yes	no
43. Lake Oswego	143	92 acres	yes	no	no
44. Harrisville Pond	146	40 acres	yes	yes	no
45. Wilson Lake	149	58 acres	yes	no	yes
46. Lake Lenape	152	350 acres	yes	no	yes
47. Lake Absegami	158	63 acres	yes	yes	yes
48. Corbin City Impoundments	161	1.3 miles	yes	no	no
49. Stewart Lake	167	45 acres	yes	no	yes
50. Parvin Lake and Thundergust Lake	170	109 acres	yes	no	no

Northern New Jersey

Northwest New Jersey includes most of the state's largest natural lakes and natural or human-made reservoirs tucked in valleys between the mountains that comprise part of the Appalachian Ridge and Valley Region and the Piedmont Plateau. Creeks and streams along the western edge of the state drain into the Delaware River. From the central and eastern portions of the state, they drain into the Hudson River or the Atlantic Ocean.

The Appalachian Trail traverses the crest of the Kittatinny Ridge in the northwest corner of the state, where black bears, coyotes, and bobcats are seen frequently. Limestone, shale, siltstone, sandstone, and gneiss compose most of the rock types here, along with smaller amounts of quartzite and schist. Volcanic activity during continental rifting left behind the durable basalt of the Watchung and Orange Mountains and the Palisades Sill. Geologically recent ice ages carved out numerous glacial lakes, such as Hopatcong and Swartswood, which are now fed by winter snowmelts and natural runoff. Glaciers once deeply gouged the valley now occupied by Lake Aeroflex.

Population density on New Jersey's eastern side, across the Hudson River from New York City, is the highest in the state. Cities such as Newark, Jersey City, and Patterson meld together as one and extend their urban sprawl farther west each year. Conservation of undisturbed lands in and around this vicinity is critical for wildlife habitat preservation.

Steeny Kill and Sawmill Lakes
High Point (Sussex)

MAPS: New Jersey Atlas & Gazetteer, Map 19
USGS Quadrangle, Point Jervis South (NY)

AREA: Steeny Kill Lake, 30 acres
Sawmill Lake, 20 acres

CAMPING AND INFORMATION: High Point State Park, 1480
State Route 23, Sussex, NJ 07461-3605; 973-875-4800. One
tenting area is found on the shore of Sawmill Lake.

HABITAT TYPE: dense woodland

EXPECT TO SEE: waterfowl, eagles and hawks, foxes, turtles,
possibly bears

TAKE NOTE: You are in bear country. Take appropriate
precautions with your food stores if you camp or hike here.
No gas engines.

GETTING THERE

Drive north on Route 23 out of Colesville for about 2.4 miles to the park
office, located on the left side of the road. To reach Sawmill Lake, proceed
another 0.5 mile past the park office, then turn left and follow the main road
for 1.8 miles to the lake. The launch site and parking areas are designated.

The Steeny Kill Lake entrance is 1.6 miles northwest of the park
office on the right-hand side of Route 23 (1.1 miles north of the
entrance to Sawmill Lake). It's only a short drive off the road to the
launch site and parking area.

A small fee is charged in summer at the park's recreational site
across the road from the visitor center, but access to both lakes is free.
Wildlife, artifact, and geologic exhibits in the center are worth a visit.

On the drive along Route 23 to High Point State Park in the extreme
northwest corner of the state, be prepared for some steep hills. This
mountainous region lies within the Appalachian Ridge and Valley Region.
As you can guess by the park's name, you will find in its boundaries the

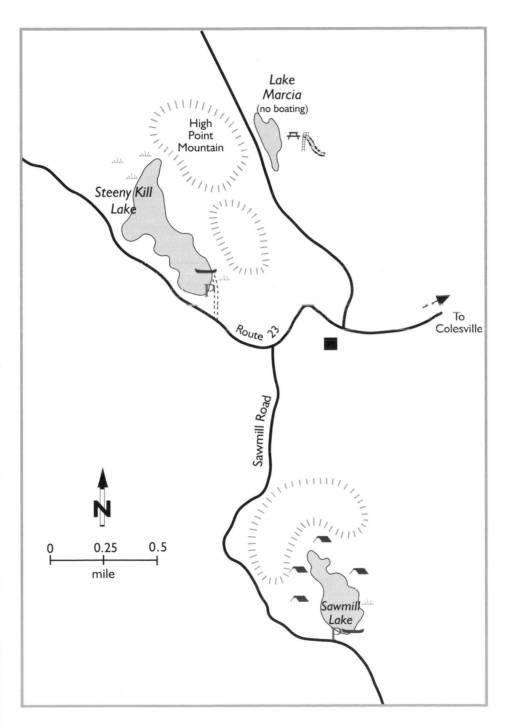

Steeny Kill and Sawmill Lakes

A view of the campsites along the eastern shore of Sawmill Lake.

highest elevation in the state, which is marked by a 220-foot monument. High Point Mountain rises 1,804 feet above sea level—not much by "real" mountain standards, but it's ours. High Point Mountain is part of the Appalachian Trail, a continuous footpath that starts at Springer Mountain in Georgia and passes through this park on the way to its northern terminus at Katahdin in Maine—a distance of more than 2,000 miles!

At the visitor center pick up maps and pamphlets that show hiking trails, campgrounds, roads to the two lakes, and directions to the High Point monument. Gas engines are prohibited at both lakes, and the only swimming beach is on Lake Marcia, which is not open to boating. More than 15 miles of mixed-use trails weave through the park, some of them possessing moderately steep sections over rocky terrain.

Black bears, bobcats, deer, and foxes are among the wildlife found inside the park's hardwood and conifer forests. At 30 acres, Steeny Kill Lake is the larger of the two lakes. Hickory, beech, and red maple prevail in the more open areas on the south shore. I personally prefer Steeny Kill Lake for kayaking—not because it's larger, but because it has an irregular shoreline with more nooks and crannies to explore. If you enjoy birding, keep alert for Cooper's and red-shouldered hawks. Bog and wood turtles inhabit the swampy southern end of the lake.

Sawmill Lake lies at the bottom of a depression on the south side of High Point Mountain. The 20-acre lake is roughly elliptical, with a few coves on the eastern and southern shores. Tall pine, oak, and hickory dominate the woods around the lake, and rustic tent sites and a few cabins sit along the eastern lakeshore. It was here that I ended my day. Before retiring, I paddled out to the middle of the lake, sat under a quarter moon, and watched the stars while frogs called to each other in the night. It was August, and the Perseid meteor showers graced me with two shooting stars—the end of a perfect day.

Lake Aeroflex, Gardner's Pond, Twin Lakes, and Whites Pond
Newton (Sussex)

MAPS: New Jersey Atlas & Gazetteer, Map 24
　　USGS Quadrangle, Newton East
AREA: Lake Aeroflex, 117 acres
　　Gardner's Pond, ~15 acres
　　Twin Lakes, ~20 acres
　　Whites Pond, ~8 acres
CAMPING: Columbia Valley Campground, 3 Ghost Pony Road,
　　Andover, NJ 07821; 973-691-0596
INFORMATION: Kittatinny Valley State Park, P.O. Box 621,
　　Andover, NJ 07821-0521; 973-786-6445
HABITAT TYPE: open woodland and fields
EXPECT TO SEE: waterfowl, hawks and eagles, turtles,
　　otters, foxes
TAKE NOTE: no motors

GETTING THERE

To Lake Aeroflex and Gardner's Pond: Take Exit 25 off I-80; drive north for about 7.0 miles on Route 206 to Andover, where Routes 517 and 613 intersect. Continue north for 0.7 mile on Route 206 to Route 669 (Limecrest Road); turn right onto Limecrest Road and drive 1.1 miles to the Kittatinny Valley State Park entrance on the left. The visitor center, boat ramp, parking, and picnic tables are within 200 feet of the entrance.

　　To Twin Lakes and Whites Pond: From its intersection with Route 669, continue for 0.9 mile on Route 206 north, then turn right onto Goodale Road and drive for 0.6 mile to the fenced entrance on the left. Drive across the parking area to the short gravel road leading to the launch site. On your way to Twin Lakes you will pass Whites Pond, which is also available for paddling; it's on the right about halfway up Goodale Road.

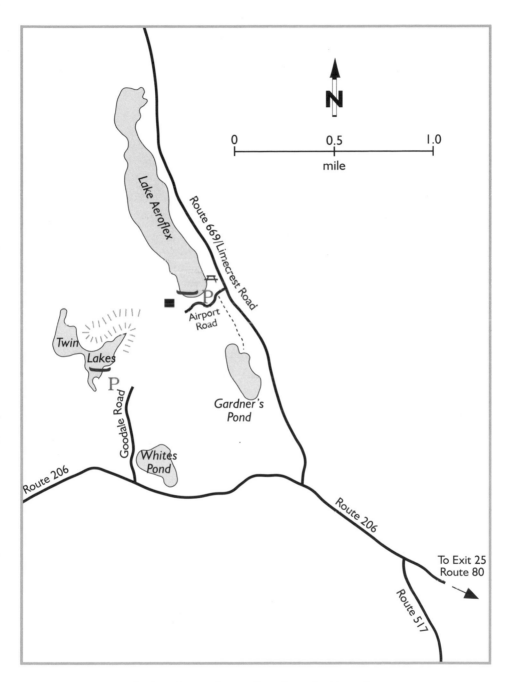

Lake Aeroflex, Gardner's Pond,
Twin Lakes, and Whites Pond

Four bodies of water reside within Kittatinny Valley State Park. One of them, Lake Aeroflex, is—at a depth of 110 feet—reportedly the deepest natural glacial lake in the state. Situated just outside the mountainous Appalachian Ridge and Valley Region, the land here starts giving way to the gentle rolling hills of the Piedmont Plateau.

Large horse and agricultural farms become more frequent as you drive through the countryside. Aeroflex-Andover airport sits between Lake Aeroflex and Gardner's Pond. Normally I would stay away from airports, but this is a small local facility with infrequent activity. Somehow the small planes taking off or landing lend an air of adventure to the setting. No air traffic can be heard from Twin Lakes or Whites Pond, located on the other side of the park.

Lake Aeroflex stretches its long and narrow 117 acres parallel to Limecrest Road (Route 669) on the northwest side of the quiet town of Andover. Ducks and geese are abundant on the shallower western shores, where clumps of aquatic grasses provide ideal foraging. Bog and painted turtles frequently sun themselves along the banks, and snapping turtles hide in the sediment on the lake bottom. Trees along the eastern shore between the lake and Limecrest Road afford visual and auditory screening from the sparse road traffic. About eight picnic tables are scattered under large trees in the open area adjacent to the park office and launching ramp. No one was on the lake when I paddled it, although local construction workers used the picnic area during their lunch break and a young mother took her two children for a brief stroll around the grounds. Swimming and motors are not permitted on any waters within the park, and only Lake Aeroflex has picnic facilities.

Gardner's Pond is located at the southern end of the airport. Only airport vehicular traffic is allowed along the road, but you can carry your boat or use a portable wheeled cart to travel 0.5 mile to the launch. It was dusk by the time I finished kayaking Lake Aeroflex and Twin Lakes, preventing further investigation. A local fisherman came from the pond and remarked, "The fishin's good, but the pond is kinda small." Perhaps next time I'll explore it.

Twin Lakes provides quaint paddling waters, where a couple of local swans may accompany you. Two bodies of water connected by a narrow neck not far from the launch site give this lake an hourglass shape. About 0.25 mile from the launch, you can choose to go right or left. The right side leads you to waters where short hills rise steeply from the shore. This is a great place to watch for belted kingfishers,

At 110 feet, Lake Aeroflex is the deepest natural glacial lake in New Jersey.

which build nests in cavities along the steep embankments a few feet above the water's surface. I spotted three in the short time I paddled this section, along with numerous frogs and spotted turtles. The brightly colored northern red salamander hides under logs on shore.

Whites Pond and the surrounding land, which had been purchased with Green Acre funds, is now open to the public.

~ 3 ~

Hackensack Meadows
Secaucus (Hudson)

MAPS: New Jersey Atlas & Gazetteer, Maps 32 and 33
USGS Quadrangles, Weehawken and Jersey City
LENGTH: open (part of the Hackensack River)
HABITAT TYPE: coastal marsh; part of the Atlantic flyway
EXPECT TO SEE: waterfowl, herons, egrets, ospreys, muskrats, turtles
TAKE NOTE: tides; winds; motorboats

GETTING THERE

Unless you're used to congested traffic, the first thing you'll want to do is have directions written out, large and legible, by your side. There is rarely a place to pull over and refer to a book; traffic is moving at a chaotic pace.

From east of Newark, take Route 78 east and get off at Exit 58B onto Pulaski Skyway (Routes 1/9) north. Look for signs that read Last Exit Before Toll. Stay in the left-hand lane, following signs for Tonnele Avenue. Exit at the Tonnele/Lincoln Tunnel—stay to the right coming off the exit. At the bottom of the ramp, you will be at a circle. Stay right around the circle (about a quarter of the way around), following signs for Routes 1/9 north (Tonnele Avenue). Look for Manhattan Street 0.6 mile down Tonnele Avenue, and get in the right-hand lane to take the jug-handle onto County Road, 0.1 mile past Manhattan (you will have to make a left-hand turn from the right-hand lane). Okay, you can breathe now, you're almost there.

Follow County Road to the T, about 2.5 miles, and turn left onto New County Road. A few blocks down, the road will bend to the right. Look for the Hudson County Park at Laurel Hill sign on the left about 200 feet past the bend; turn left into the park and follow signs to the boat launch on the right. You made it!

You're probably thinking, "Secaucus? This is supposed to be a book on good *quiet* paddling sites!" I'm sure you think it crazy to suggest paddling

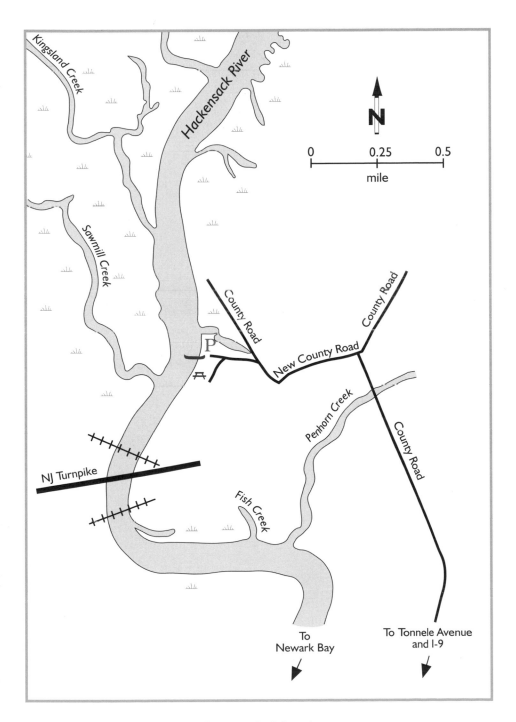

Hackensack Meadows

anywhere in this highly industrialized, overly populated area. For those living nearby, however, Hackensack Meadows offers one of the few spots to paddle within a reasonable distance. It also helps us realize how important it is to protect such precious environments for wildlife and public enjoyment in the midst of highly developed cities. I also admit the desire to find at least one decent paddling location in every New Jersey county, even tiny Hudson County.

The Hackensack Riverkeeper Canoe Project's main goal is to have Hackensack Meadows designated as a national wildlife reserve to protect it from further development. The organization maintains a base of operation in a small trailer next to the boat ramp, where they rent canoes, run eco-cruises, organize river cleanups, and distribute literature to foster public awareness of this valuable environment.

Migrating birds use the meadows to rest and feed before continuing their journeys. Some stay to grace the state with their presence throughout the warmer months, and a few become year-round residents in this rich estuarine environment where the Hackensack River winds through the marshes. Birds frequently seen here include egrets, herons, yellowlegs, stilt and semipalmated sandpipers, least and Forster's terns, and black skimmers. Watch the terns as they hunt for prey, hovering in place 20 to 40 feet above the water, then plunging straight down for the catch. Scan the mud flats carefully for the occasional avocet, and the grassy shallows for common moorhen. Look carefully at the edges of marsh grass for yellow- and black-crowned night-herons, a delightful find. Paddle up and down the river and inspect side channels where feeder streams enter; wading birds are often found there.

The Hackensack River is a few hundred yards wide here and, with nothing but open salt marshes all around, can churn up pretty well on a windy day. Keep alert to changes in weather and observe the same caution here as you would on a large lake. From the boat launch, the best paddling is to the right (upriver), where numerous feeder streams and small creeks offer hours of exploration. Look carefully at the grassy corners for the gnawed, telltale sign of muskrat activity, then see if you can find their mounded house about 15 feet or so back from the water.

The diamondback terrapin, *Malaclemys terrapin*, is the only turtle in the continental United States that is found solely in brackish saltwater environments. Aside from habitat, concentric rings or ridges on its shell, along with a spotted head and limbs, confirm this reptile's identification. Females can attain a length of 9 inches, but males reach

Great egrets search for food in the shallow waters of a channel leading off the Hackensack River.

only 5.5 inches. I haven't heard of many sightings here, since they are highly susceptible to pollution—another good reason to support efforts to have this site designated a national wildlife reserve. For further information, contact Hackensack Riverkeeper Inc. in residence at Fairleigh Dickinson University, 1000 River Road–T090C, Teaneck, NJ 07666; 201-692-8440.

If you go left (downstream) from the ramp, do not go past the third bridge (ignore railroad bridges) about 3.0 miles down. It becomes heavily industrialized, and you'll be within 4.0 miles of Newark Bay, where tidal currents strengthen.

~4~

Pompton Lake
Pompton Lakes (Passaic)

> **MAPS:** New Jersey Atlas & Gazetteer, Map 26
>   USGS Quadrangles, Wanaque and Pompton Plains
> **AREA:** 204 acres
> **INFORMATION:** New Jersey Division of Fish and Wildlife,
>   Northern Region Office, 26 Route 173 West, Hampton,
>   NJ 08827; 973-383-0918
> **HABITAT TYPE:** urban; open woods
> **EXPECT TO SEE:** ducks, geese, and other waterfowl
> **TAKE NOTE:** motorboats, but limited to 10 HP

GETTING THERE

From the South: Take Route 202 north into the town of Pompton Lakes, where it becomes part of the Patterson–Hamburg Turnpike. Route 202 turns right in the center of town onto Terhune Drive; continue north for 0.9 mile on Route 202 (Terhune Drive). The park entrance will be on the left, 50 feet past Lamoureaux Lane, which will be on the right. The entrance to the park is tricky, because signs are not visible until you are almost at the narrow entrance road flanked by large stone pillars. The boat ramp is on the right side of the parking area. If the ramp gate is closed, you can carry your boat from the parking lot to the water, a distance of about 100 feet.

From the North: Take Route 287 to Exit 58 and drive south on Route 202 for about 2.9 miles to Lakeside Avenue, which crosses over the lake on the right. Drive 0.3 mile past Lakeside Avenue to the park entrance on the right.

The majority of lakeside property on Pompton Lake is privately owned, but most of the houses are on large properties set back from the shoreline and screened by trees, providing pleasant paddling conditions. Willow scattered along the shore drape delicate branches that shimmer with the slightest breeze. Ducks, geese, and swans forage among vegetation in shallow waters of this long, 204-acre lake. Paddle

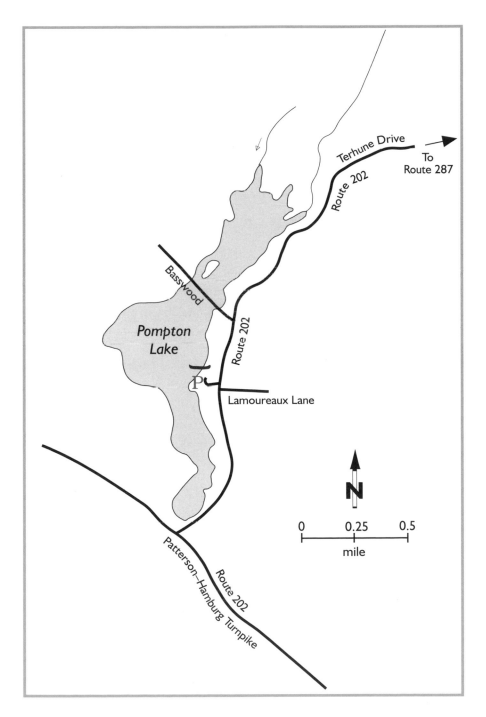

Pompton Lake

A duck floats on the waters of Pompton Lake.

to the northern end of the lake from the put-in to circle a small island on the west side immediately past the bridge at Lakeside Avenue.

Pompton Lake can be accessed from the public boat launch in Terhune Memorial Park on the eastern side of the lake. For a lunch break, stop at the picnic tables or the small pagoda situated close to the water's edge under the huge park trees. While motorboats are permitted on the lake, a 10-horsepower limit is imposed. Swimming is not allowed.

～ 5 ～

Shepherd Lake
Ringwood (Passaic)

MAPS: New Jersey Atlas & Gazetteer, Map 21
   USGS Quadrangle, Sloatsburg
AREA: 74 acres
INFORMATION: Ringwood State Park, 1304 Sloatsburg Road,
   Ringwood, NJ 07456; 973-962-7031
HABITAT TYPE: thick upland woods
EXPECT TO SEE: foxes, eagles, hawks
TAKE NOTE: You are in bear country. Take appropriate precautions if you hike the many trails. Electric motorboats only.

GETTING THERE

From the south, take Exit 55 off I-287, drive north for 7.3 miles on Route 511 (Ringwood Avenue), and turn right onto Sloatsburg Road. Beautiful Wanaque Reservoir will be on the left—no boating is allowed on the reservoir. Drive 2.3 miles on Sloatsburg Road, turn right onto Morris Road, and continue for 1.4 miles. At the intersection a sign directs you to Shepherd Lake on the left, about 1.0 mile down the road. Signs also point straight ahead to the Botanical Gardens less than 0.25 mile away. Stay to the right after the tollbooth for the boat ramp and parking area. A small entrance fee is charged between Memorial Day and Labor Day to cover the cost of seasonal help, but off-season access is free.

Tucked snuggly in the northeast corner of Ringwood State Park along the New York border, the 74-acre Shepherd Lake is completely enclosed by hills densely packed with stately pine, hemlock, and various hardwoods. Pink mountain laurel brighten the woods during early summer, and large maple and poplar jutting out between dense evergreens create a magnificent palette of fall colors. As you drive the mountainous road to the lake, look for large boulders, called erratics, which dot the landscape: remnants of the last ice age.

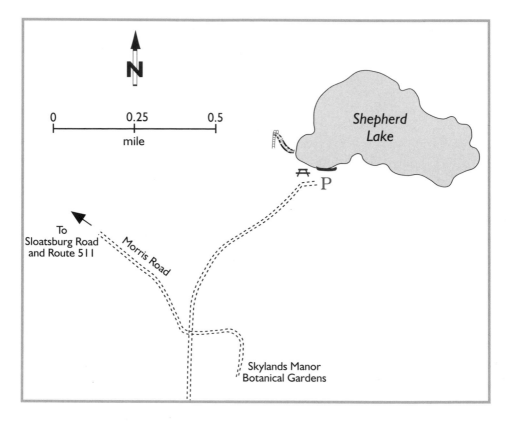

Shepherd Lake

Around the shoreline toward the east end of the lake you will quickly lose sight of the bathing beach and enjoy exploring big coves and little inlets framed by hemlock, pine, and maple. Gulls visiting the lake dive for fish in the clear, spring-fed waters, and blue jays screech their way through the surrounding forest. On open lakes like this, keep your eyes peeled for soaring eagles and hawks. Fishing is excellent throughout the lake; trout, pickerel, and largemouth bass are the primary catch of most anglers. These spring-fed mountain waters remain quite brisk throughout summer, so be wary of hypothermia, and always bring adequate clothing along even on the hottest days.

Miles of hiking trails surround the lake and meander through the park. Contact the New York–New Jersey Trail Conference at 212-685-9699 for a trail map of the park. If you desire to venture out on a long hike, make sure you have a map, compass, water, and snacks. Let someone know that you are hiking, and your intended route.

Rocky shorelines and hemlock are typical of mountain lakes.

Only electric outboards are permitted on the lake. Picnic tables, a basketball court, food concessions, and a small playground surround the open recreation area next to the swimming beach on the southwest corner of the lake. Sadly, there is no camping available inside the park.

Ringwood State Park and its surrounding lands once housed important iron-producing complexes during the industry's heyday in the eighteenth and nineteenth centuries. From the mid-1700s the Ringwood Company's iron forges and furnaces supplied the colonies with products for more than a hundred years and contributed to war efforts during the American Revolution, the War of 1812, and the Civil War. Ringwood Manor, a forty-one-room mansion located inside the park, was home to the local ironmasters.

If you have time, I recommend stopping at the unique Botanical Gardens at Skylands Manor. You will pass a sign pointing to the gardens on the way to Shepherd Lake. A Tudor-style manor house at the entrance serves as an information center and the hub for local horticultural clubs. Marked serpentine roads meander through 96 acres of natural and formal wildflower gardens, trees, shrubs, and bogs. Most of the roads are one-way, encouraging a leisurely drive, but biking or walking are the best ways to enjoy these magnificent gardens.

～6～
Monksville Reservoir
West Milford (Passaic)

MAPS: New Jersey Atlas & Gazetteer, Map 20
USGS Quadrangles, Greenwood Lake and Wanaque
AREA: 505 acres
INFORMATION: Long Pond Ironworks State Park, Route 511,
Greenwood Lake Turnpike, Ringwood, NJ; 201-962-7031
HABITAT TYPE: some woods, some open areas
EXPECT TO SEE: hawks, eagles, waterfowl
TAKE NOTE: motorboats (to 10 HP); winds

GETTING THERE

There are two boat ramps on the reservoir. From the south, take Exit 55 off I-287 and drive north on Route 511 (Ringwood Avenue) for about 7.0 miles to Sloatsburg Road on the right. Continue on Route 511 for another 1.3 miles to Stonetown Road on the left. The first gated entrance is on the left 0.3 mile north of Stonetown Road. A second gated entrance, again on the left, can be found at the other end of the reservoir, 0.7 mile north on Route 511 past the first gate. Both areas have ample parking

Both launch sites have well-maintained portable toilets. A 10-horsepower limit is imposed on all motorboats, but weekends during prime fishing season may be a little noisy in the early-morning hours when most anglers head for their favorite spots. Swimming is not permitted.

Want a nice long paddle and some great fishing? Then visit the 505-acre Monksville Reservoir, which encircles Long Pond Ironworks State Park like a giant horseshoe. You'll find the most interesting paddling on the far side of the reservoir, where coves of all sizes form a continuous string along the highly irregular shoreline. White birches seem particularly abundant around the lake, contrasting sharply against dark evergreens. Ducks and geese can be found around the lake in the protected coves. Of all the fish that inhabit these waters, the big muskellunge is the most

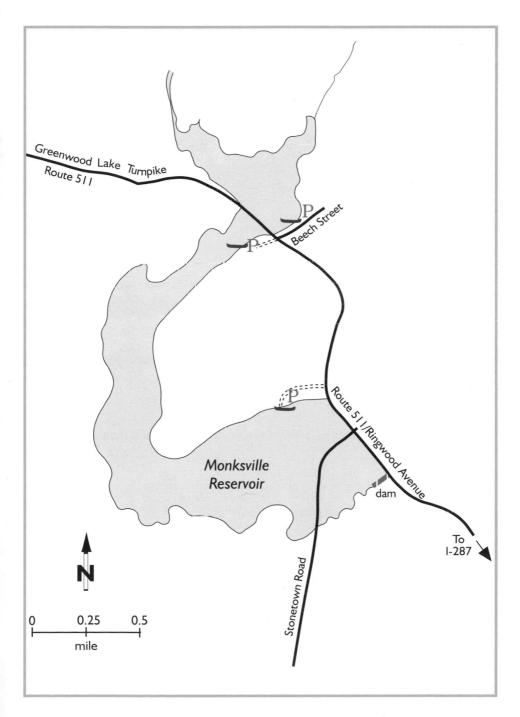

Greenwood Lake Turnpike
Route 511

P

P

Beech Street

P

Route 511/Ringwood Avenue

Monksville
Reservoir

dam

Stonetown Road

To
I-287

N

0   0.25   0.5
mile

Monksville Reservoir

A rocky ledge faces the northern launch site from across the lake.

sought after by anglers. Prehistoric-looking snapping turtles inhabit the lake but are seen rarely, because they spend most of their time underwater (unlike other turtles, which like to bask in the sun).

The northern end of the reservoir passes under the bridge at Route 511 and the scenery changes to a shallower, more marshlike environment. That's what I like about paddling under bridges: I just might be surprised by something different on the other side. To the left, a large field of drowned trees sticks out of shallow waters, inviting you to weave in and out looking for turtles sunning themselves on low stumps. Dense clumps of aquatic grasses create perfect nursery grounds for large lake fish. Bird watching here is also quite different; warblers and finches visibly flit about, and pileated woodpeckers nest in cavities of dead trees. To the right, a small boat shed on a wooden dock rents canoes. Open grassy areas invite you to pull up, stop for lunch, and stretch your legs.

Long Pond Iron Works historical site, located just north of the reservoir on Route 511, offers visitors the opportunity to tour the ruins of three furnaces and buildings of the old iron-smelting complex. Peter Hasenclever founded the operation in 1766. It was run by a succession of famous ironmasters, including Robert Erskin and Abram Hewitt, for almost 200 years. The park is listed on the State and National Registers of Historic Places.

~ 7 ~

Green Turtle Pond
West Milford (Passaic)

MAPS: New Jersey Atlas & Gazetteer, Map 20
  USGS Quadrangle, Greenwood Lake
AREA: 40 acres
INFORMATION: North Jersey District Water Supply Commission,
  1 F. A. Orechio Drive, Wanaque, NJ 07465; 973-836-3600
HABITAT TYPE: primarily dense woods
EXPECT TO SEE: waterfowl, eagles, hawks, foxes, turtles
TAKE NOTE: electric motors only

GETTING THERE

Starting on Greenwood Lake Turnpike in West Milford, drive south for 0.8 mile on Route 511, then turn left onto Awosting Road. Be careful here—this is a hairpin turn. Drive 0.6 mile on Awosting Road to the wildlife management area entrance. A large sign is at the entrance, but it sits back from the road partially hidden by trees. The best bet is to look for two stone pillars, one on each side of the road, about 500 feet before the entrance. Each pillar is approximately 3 feet square and 5 feet high. Once partially blacktopped, the steep road leading down to the lake is now extremely potholed. The road widens near the lake, providing ample parking.

Don't miss this gem! Driving down the steep, potholed road to the lake for the first time, I came around the last bend and stepped on the brakes. Islands, two of them, jutted out of the water a couple of hundred yards offshore from the dirt-and-stone ramp ahead; I couldn't wait to get my kayak into the water. Islands not only provide more shoreline to explore, but also visually break up the lake's surface, creating a feeling of adventure. At the sound of my car creeping toward the ramp, a female mallard, 10 feet away, quickly escorted her brood toward dense shrubs farther along the edge; I had disturbed their tranquil swim.

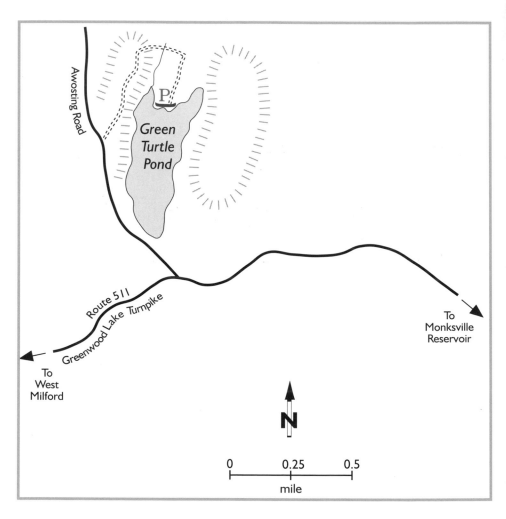

Green Turtle Pond

Tucked in a valley with steep mountains on three sides, this is a great place to come on windy days. On either side of the ramp, cedar and red maple can be seen among aquatic plants and grasses. Turkey vultures soar on warm thermals of air along the steep mountainside on the northern edge of the lake. Only one other boat was on the lake that first day, an electric outboard with two anglers. We nodded in recognition, but exchanged no words.

Several narrow animal paths lead to the lake, and you can usually spot a number of deer. Two dead trees on the larger island showed

Just a few hundred yards south of the launch site you'll have the opportunity to explore two islands.

evidence of recent woodpecker activity, because the wood was not weathered looking; perhaps one had nested there earlier that summer. The rocky outcroppings on the island's north end may harbor timber rattlesnakes or northern copperheads, both of which are poisonous. Exercise caution if you climb the hills.

Camping around the lake is the only thing missing here. Only electric outboards are permitted on the lake, which is located inside Wanaque Wildlife Management Area. There's also no formal swimming beach, picnic tables, or facilities of any kind—just the dirt-and-stone ramp leading to a pristine environment. Go for it!

Wawayanda Lake
Vernon (Sussex)

MAPS: New Jersey Atlas & Gazetteer, Map 20
  USGS Quadrangle, Wawayanda

AREA: 255 acres

CAMPING AND INFORMATION: Wawayanda State Park, 885
  Warwick Turnpike, Hewitt, NJ 07421; 973-853-4468

HABITAT TYPE: primarily wooded with some open areas

EXPECT TO SEE: waterfowl, wading birds, eagles, hawks, otters,
  foxes, deer, bears

TAKE NOTE: You are in bear country. Take appropriate precautions if you hike or camp. It can be windy here as well.
  Electric outboards only.

GETTING THERE

Drive south for 0.2 mile on Route 23 from Route 171 to the Clinton Road exit. Drive north on Clinton Road for about 7.0 miles until you come to the T-junction at Route 513 (Warwick Turnpike). Turn left (north) onto Route 513 and drive for 2.3 miles to the park entrance on the left. Stop at the visitor center to pick up a map and other useful pamphlets. From the visitor center, continue for 1.9 miles to the turn-off for the recreation area. The road to the boat launch will be on the left. The park is open from 6 A.M. to 8 P.M. Parking is available at the launch site.

Nestled within the vast mountains of Wawayanda State Park, this large mountain lake will provide days of enjoyable paddling. Camping is available, but I advise making reservations if you intend to visit during summer. Picnic grounds, a sandy bathing beach, a playground, and boat rentals all are situated at the large recreational area on the north side of the lake. Weekends in July and August can be extremely crowded with hikers, anglers, and vacationers.

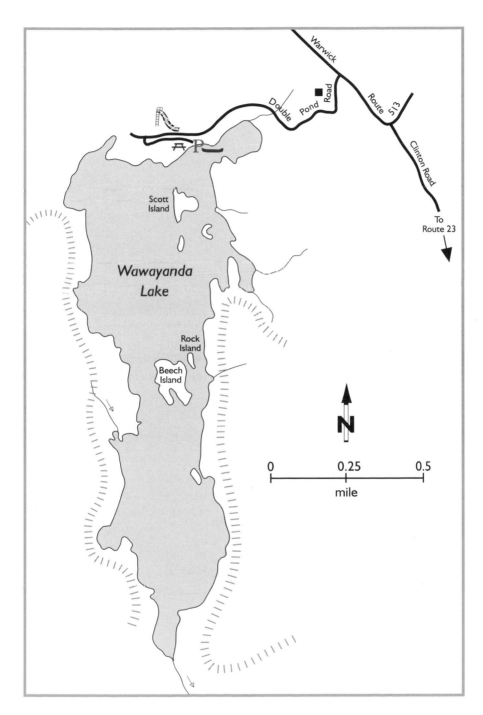

Warwick

Double Pond Road

Route 513

Clinton Road

To
Route 23

Scott
Island

Wawayanda
Lake

Rock
Island

Beech
Island

N

0   0.25   0.5
mile

Wawayanda Lake

I camped here in August for two weekdays, but cool winds were blowing a little more than 12 miles an hour both days, possibly keeping many from engaging in beach activities or paddling. Later in the day, winds gusting to 16 MPH over the large, 255-acre lake created small whitecaps. Several deep coves and half a dozen islands provide a welcome shelter from vigorous paddling conditions on windy days. Duck into a cove or around to the lee side of an island for a rest if you encounter adverse conditions.

Other than self-propelled boats, only quiet electric outboards are permitted. You can escape the more populated recreation areas next to the launch site by paddling toward the southern end of this long lake. Distance and tree-covered islands will soon block most audible sounds of civilization. Though a multitude of canoes are available for rent, most people do not venture past the middle of the lake, making the southern end more peaceful.

Wawayanda Lake is a good place to try your luck at fishing. Depths range from just a few feet close to shore to about 90 feet in the center of the northern half. Trout, largemouth bass, catfish, yellow perch, and large sunfish swim beneath the surface, any one of which would taste delicious cooked over a campfire at day's end. One fish with a long history on earth, the bowfin, also can be found in the lake. Look

Kayakers take a leisurely paddle toward one of the lake's large islands.

closely in the long, shallow inlets and you might be lucky enough to see a river otter.

Hiking and biking trails meander for more than 40 miles throughout 12,000 acres of Atlantic white cedar swamps and hardwood forests here. Wood and bog turtles inhabit swampy areas along with raccoons, possums, and skunks. A 20-mile stretch of the Appalachian Trail runs along the western boundary, crossing deep ravines and climbing to sensational mountaintop views. Watch out for rattlesnakes and copperheads when hiking the trails—they often warm themselves on sunny rocks or ground. Throughout the park, birdlife is bountiful. Red-shouldered hawks, great blue herons, vultures, eagles, warblers, orioles, and various songbirds are around if you are observant.

Start out early in the morning for the most peaceful paddling. That's also the best time to check out the bird populations and look for other wildlife such as raccoons, coyotes, gray foxes, and deer, which are most active just after dawn.

Bear-crossing signs posted on many roads should help you remember to be careful about food while camping. Seal all containers tightly, and put them in your car when you're finished eating. An excellent pamphlet on do's and don'ts while in bear country is available at the visitor center. Get it. Read it.

Bowfin

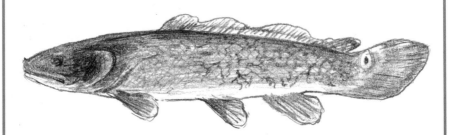

The only extant representative of the family Amiidae, bowfin date back to the early-Jurassic period about 100 million years ago when dinosaurs roamed the earth. A bony gular plate located between the jaws on its underside is a distinctive characteristic of this olive-colored fish with a long, low dorsal fin and a partially lobed caudal fin (tail). Males have a black spot ringed with yellow or orange at the upper base of the tail; females have a similar spot but no ring. Hard plates in the mouth wreak havoc on anglers' hooks, and bowfin's sharp teeth can cut through line—and fingers—readily. Like gar, bowfin have a modified air bladder that enables them to breathe surface air and thus tolerate stagnant, oxygen-depleted waters.

Although the majority of the extinct bowfin forms were marine, the modern bowfin is restricted to the sluggish-moving streams and backwaters of eastern North America, the same environment as bass and crappies. Voracious feeders, bowfin have been known to decimate local game-fish populations on occasion. Their primary diet consists of crustaceans, insects, larvae, and small fish. Adults attain lengths of 18 to 42 inches and can reach weights of up to 20 pounds. While considered poor eating, they are sought by anglers for the feisty fight they provide. Use the same bait and tackle to catch them as you would for bass.

Bowfin breed in spring after an elaborate ritual during which they construct bowl-shaped nests by tearing out weeds in a shallow area. Once a female is attracted to the nest, spawning commences. Males guard the eggs and fry for several weeks and may mate with several females during that time, thus having eggs in various stages of development. Young are equipped with an adhesive organ on their snout that enables them to hold on to weeds and remain at the nest site. Their rapid growth rate allows them to reach lengths up to 9 inches in their first year.

～9～

Swartswood and Paulins Kill Lakes

Swartswood (Sussex)

MAPS: New Jersey Atlas & Gazetteer, Map 23
USGS Quadrangle, Newton West

AREA: Swartswood, 494 acres
Paulins Kill, ~250 acres

CAMPING: Swartswood State Park, P.O. Box 123, Swartswood, NJ 07887-0123; 973-383-5230

HABITAT TYPE: Swartswood, dense to open woods; some lake development
Paulins Kill, wooded in the northern third; lake development along the rest

EXPECT TO SEE: Swartswood, waterfowl, wading birds, song birds, water plants
Paulins Kill, large hemlock stand, waterfowl

TAKE NOTE: electric motorboats only; winds on Swartswood Lake

---

GETTING THERE

Access to Swartswood State Park is conveniently located near the junction of Routes 622 and 619 about 2.0 miles west of Route 94. From Route 619, drive west for 0.5 mile on Route 622 to the entrance for Little Swartswood Lake boat launch. To access Swartswood Lake from the same junction, drive south for 1.0 mile on Route 619 to the boat launch on the right. Maps can be picked up at the park office and visitor center, located 0.6 mile south on Route 619. The swimming beach, playground, and picnic areas are also located there.

From Route 94 in the town of Fredon, drive west for 2.3 miles on Route 614 (Paulins Kill Lake Road), turn right onto Route 619, and drive for 1.8 miles to the main park entrance on the left.

A car-top launch is available at the extreme southern end of Swartswood Lake. From Route 622, drive south for 2.3 miles on Route 521. You will see a very small Boat Launch sign on the left. The launch is 150 feet off the road,

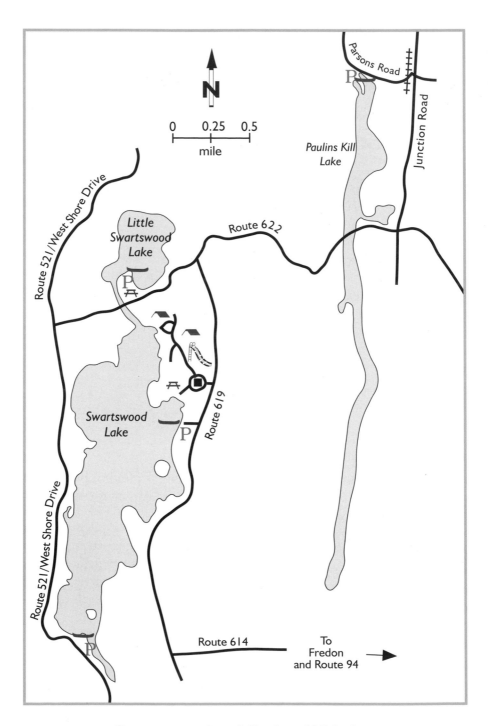

Swartswood and Paulins Kill Lakes

with parking available for about eight cars. This is a pretty spot tucked in the woods and a great spot for an informal picnic before or after your paddle.

Access to nearby Paulins Kill Lake is only a ten-minute drive from the junction of Routes 622 and 619. From Route 619, drive east for 1.9 miles on Route 622, turn left onto Junction Road and continue for 1.0 mile, then turn left onto Parsons Road. *Caution:* Immediately after turning onto Parsons Road, you will go under a very narrow railroad trestle that is little more than one car wide. Continue on Parsons Road for 0.4 mile to the roadside parking area and boat launch on the left. The small dirt clearing with a few shrubs and saplings is easily overlooked.

Swartswood and Paulins Kill Lakes in the northwest mountains of the state can be accessed through Swartswood State Park, which offers camping, picnicking, playgrounds, and swimming. Neither lake lies completely within the park's boundary, so you will find private property at various points on the south and west sides. For the most part, the houses are set back from the tree-lined shores and do not detract from the setting.

Stop at the park office on Route 619 for a map and information about camping. Tent/trailer campsites and three yurts (circular tents built on a wood frame featuring a deck and a Plexiglas skylight) are available. Swartswood Lake gives you almost 500 acres in which to paddle. Hours can be spent exploring the numerous coves and peninsulas along the perimeter. According to locals, fishing is good in both lakes, with walleye and brown trout the best catches. Mountain laurel and mulberry bushes grow in the shade of pine, oak, ash, birch, and hickory trees. Birding is excellent, with a number of observation facilities within the park: watch carefully and you might catch a glimpse of the colorful scarlet tanager. Butterflies, essential to the pollination process of many botanical species, dance from wildflower to wildflower along the sunny shores. Since the swimming beach is located at the extreme northern end, it is quite easy to escape into quieter waters by paddling south (left) from the launch. Hiking and nature trails lead through upland forests and bogs within the 1,357-acre park. A small car-top launch area is also available on the southern end of Swartswood Lake.

Looking down a small section of the three-mile–long lake.

Paulins Kill Lake is unique due to its extremely long and narrow shape. A private community gobbles up the land along its southern half. Most of the houses sit back from the shoreline, but their docks are prominent features. Only a few private properties adjoin the lake in the northern section above the Route 622 bridge where the New Jersey Division of Fish and Wildlife recently acquired a large parcel of land through the Green Acres Program. There are no recreational facilities here—just a boat ramp for a quiet paddle on the northern end. Dense stands of hemlock within mixed hardwood forests on the east hillsides are breathtaking, and the steep banks provide perfect habitat for kingfishers. A few small low-lying dirt edges allow you to stop for a lunch break or stretch your legs. I thoroughly enjoyed paddling this lake, particularly the upper portion on state-owned property. This would be a great location on windier days when you want to get a good workout, because its narrow width offers protection from all but the windiest conditions.

White's Lake
Squires Corner (Warren)

MAPS: New Jersey Atlas & Gazetteer, Map 23
    USGS Quadrangle, Flatbrookville

AREA: 70 acres

CAMPING: Triplebrook Family Camping Resort is nearby on a
    250-acre farm. Triplebrook Family Camping Resort, 58
    Honey Run Road, Blairstown, NJ 07825; 888-343-CAMP.

INFORMATION: New Jersey Division of Fish and Wildlife, North-
    ern Region Office, 26 Route 173 West, Hampton, NJ 08827;
    973-383-0918

HABITAT TYPE: some woods, some open country

EXPECT TO SEE: waterfowl

TAKE NOTE: hunting is permitted during duck season

GETTING THERE

White's Lake Natural Reserve Area is located about 5.0 miles north of
Blairstown along the east side of Route 521 (Stillwater Road), 0.4 mile north
of the Route 659 junction. A few houses at this junction compose the blink-
and-you'll-miss-it town of Squires Corner. A large Reserve Area sign is displayed prominently at the entrance to the gravel road leading to the lake and
parking area visible from Route 521.

White's Lake is totally enclosed by a natural reserve area in the rural
countryside of western Warren County. Vegetation in the narrow strip
between the lake and the road consists of tall grasses and a few saplings.
Thick stands of *Phragmites* reed on either side of the launch site provide ample screening from the road. Dense woods surround the rest of
the oval-shaped lake, with red maple and other water-loving trees more
common along the shoreline.

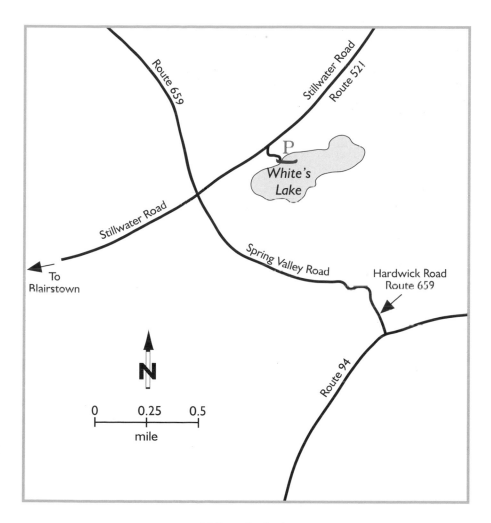

White's Lake

While not superbly scenic, White's Lake can provide a peaceful hour or two of paddling. The lake is surrounded by public property without recreational facilities. Wild carrot, butterfly weed, thistle, goldenrod, and giant sunflower color grassy borders and attract butterflies with their nectar. On the lake, painted and spotted turtles bask on fallen logs, while box turtles can be found under leaves in moist hollows on shore. Although I saw only turkey vultures, this should be a prime area to spot the hawks that frequent nearby open fields in search of small rodents.

~ 11 ~

Oxford Furnace Lake
Oxford (Warren)

MAPS: New Jersey Atlas & Gazetteer, Map 28
    USGS Quadrangle, Belvidere
AREA: 53 acres
INFORMATION: New Jersey Division of Fish and Wildlife, Northern Region Office, 26 Route 173 West, Hampton, NJ 08827; 973-383-0918
HABITAT TYPE: open woods; some development
EXPECT TO SEE: waterfowl, floating water plants

GETTING THERE

From Route 46, drive south on Route 31 for about 2.0 miles to the town of Oxford. Look for Wall Street on the right, then make the next right onto Kent Street. Drive two blocks to the T, turn left onto Route 625 for one block, then turn right onto Furnace Street. A billboard-sized sign for the newly renovated park is displayed proudly at the corner of Furnace Street and Route 625. For a small town, I found the streets a bit confusing—and changes were being made at one of the intersections. I know no one wants to do this, but, if all else fails, ask directions.

A furnace once operated in the small town of Oxford at the foot of the mountains during the heyday of the iron industry in the eighteenth and nineteenth centuries. The Green Acres Program contributed funds for the refurbishment of the 53-acre lake and surrounding property, with amenities including a soccer field, playground, picnic area, swimming beach, and boat launch. It may be noisy on weekends, but given the lack of private property on the lake, you can escape the high-use recreation areas and enjoy the rest of the scenery. Wild grape leaves weave their tendrils around trees in open areas of the south end, inviting warblers, sparrows, and golden finches to nest. This would make an excellent alternative to Merrill Creek Reservoir (half an hour's drive south; see Trip 13) on windy days.

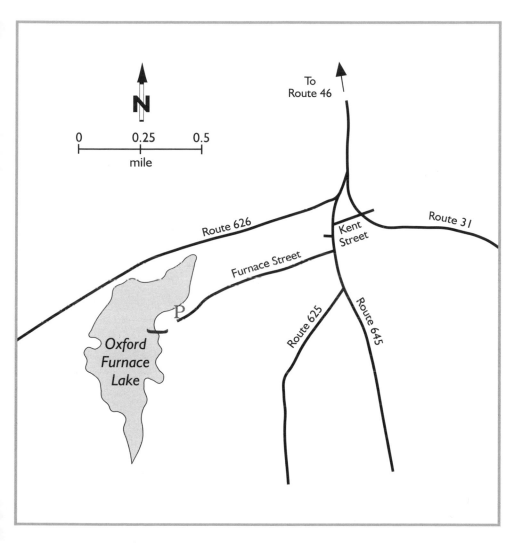

Oxford Furnace Lake

Columbia Lake

Polkville (Warren)

MAPS: New Jersey Atlas & Gazetteer, Map 22
  USGS Quadrangle, Portland

AREA: 55 acres

CAMPING: Camp Taylor Campground, 85 Mount Pleasant Road,
  Columbia, NJ 07832; 908-496-4333

INFORMATION: New Jersey Division of Fish and Wildlife, Northern Region Office, 26 Route 173 West, Hampton, NJ 08827;
  973-383-0918

HABITAT TYPE: open woods; marshes

EXPECT TO SEE: waterfowl, wading birds, marsh plants

TAKE NOTE: electric motors only

GETTING THERE

Take I-80 to Exit 4, drive north for 0.75 mile on Route 94, turn right, and drive 0.3 mile on Warrington Road. After crossing over a small bridge where Paulins Kill Creek flows into the lake, turn right onto the dirt road, and drive about 0.6 mile to the end. Because the dirt road parallels private property, it may appear to be part of a driveway. It isn't—as will become evident once you're past the house. A wooden sign for Columbia Lake is at the entrance, but it is dark with age and the lettering was barely visible when I visited. I suspect one good winter storm may knock it down.

Long, narrow, and rather shallow, Columbia Lake is the place to go for bird watching. The only drawback is the proximity to noisy I-80, but visit the 55-acre lake anyway, especially if you enjoy birding. Its long, narrow islands and hammocks offer abundant shelter for waterfowl and provide an interesting trip as you weave in and out of the serpentine maze. Since much of the lake is shallow, frogs and turtles are plentiful, particularly in the northern half. Miles of hiking trails here connect to the Appalachian Trail system.

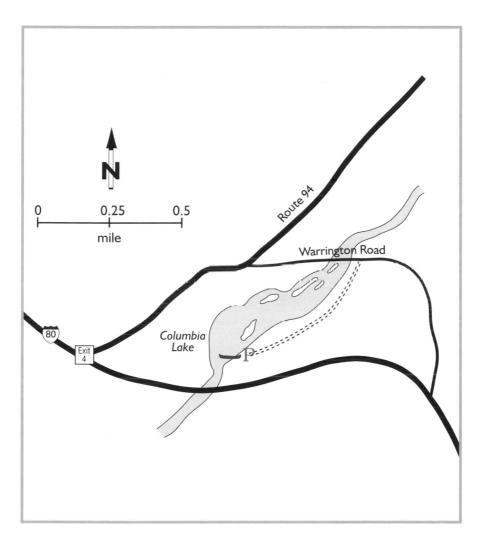

Columbia Lake

From the I-80 ramps, you get a magnificent view of the Delaware
River Water Gap—once a continuous east–west mountain ridge holding back a large inland sea. Erosion worked on a weak spot, however,
gradually wearing it down until the waters started to escape. After the
outflow started, erosion accelerated, eventually creating a channel that
would later become part of the Delaware River channel.

～ 13 ～

Merrill Creek Reservoir
Stewartsville (Warren)

Maps: New Jersey Atlas & Gazetteer, Map 28
   USGS Quadrangle, Bloomsbury
Area: 650 acres
Information: New Jersey Division of Fish and Wildlife,
   Northern Region Office, 26 Route 173 West, Hampton, NJ
   08827; 973-383-0918
Habitat Type: mostly dense woods with a few open areas
Expect to See: waterfowl, eagles, hawks, deer, foxes
Take Note: electric motor boats only; winds

GETTING THERE

Take Exit 3 off I-78, following signs for Route 22. Drive west for 0.6 mile on Route 22 and exit onto Route 519 north. Drive north for about 4.2 miles on Route 519 and turn right (north) onto Route 647 (Harmony Brass Castle Road). From there, keep track of the mile markers and turn right onto Montana Road just past Mile Marker 5. Two miles down the road will be a T; turn right onto Richline Road and drive for 0.7 mile to the entrance of the preserve. This is not necessarily the quickest way, but it is the easiest (and safest) way to get there. Signs at the entrance will direct you to the visitor center; or you can follow the Boat Launch signs straight ahead to go directly to the ramp.

From the north, drive south on Route 647 from Route 623, a few miles south of Oxford. Keep track of the mile markers and slow down as you near Mile Marker 5. Montana Road will be on the left, just before you get to Mile Marker 5. Continue as above.

I found Merrill Creek Reservoir to be the least scenic (but still very nice) of the three large reservoirs in the area—the others are Spruce Run (Trip 26) and Round Valley (Trip 25)—but at 650 acres it provides for a full day of exploration. Long stretches of dead trees rimming the shoreline near the launch did not make an appealing first impression,

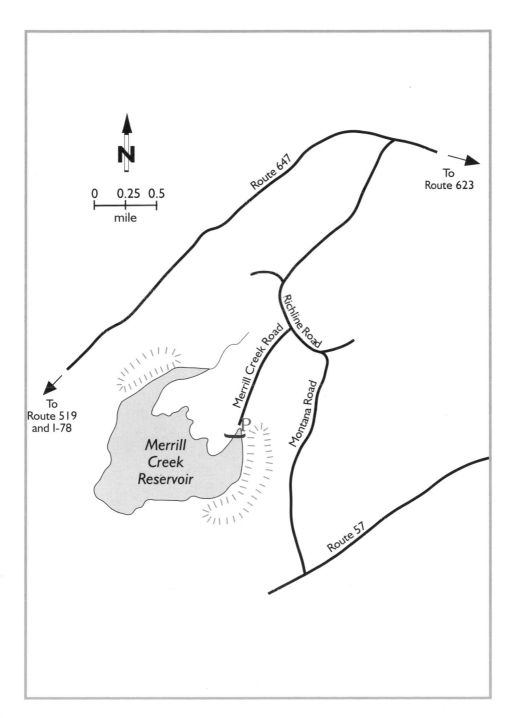

Merrill Creek Reservoir

Check for woodpecker activity in the dead trees that rim the reservoir.

but once you're away from that area the scenery improves. There's no fee, even in summer, but there is a minimum length requirement for kayaks and canoes—9 feet and 12 feet, respectively.

Most of the shoreline is smooth, but if you paddle left from the launch site, a few large coves will spice up your paddling adventures. The water depth extends to 200 feet, so if you fish, make sure you have plenty of line on the reel. Largemouth and smallmouth bass, and brown and rainbow trout are the primary species preferred by anglers. Lights on two towers flash when winds exceed 25 miles per hour for five seconds or more, and all boats must head back to the launch. Sitting atop a mountain where vigorous winds can prevail, the warning lights provide an excellent safety measure. More than 2,000 acres of forested hills and mountains supply hikers and birders with miles of trails, one of which leads out from the northeast corner of the parking lot to a crest overlooking the reservoir. Maps can be picked up at the visitor center near the entrance. Swimming and camping are not permitted within the preserve.

~14~

Lakes Hopatcong and Musconetcong
Lake Hopatcong and Netcong (Morris/Sussex)

MAPS: New Jersey Atlas & Gazetteer, Map 24
  USGS Quadrangles, Dover and Stanhope
AREA: Lake Hopatcong, 2,685 acres
  Lake Musconetcong, 329 acres
CAMPING: Mahlon Dickerson Reservation off Exit 34B of I-80.
  Take Route 15 north for 5.0 miles to the Weldon Road exit,
  then drive east on Weldon Road for 3.5 miles. This is a
  3,000-acre county park with wooded sites. Mahlon Dickerson
  Reservation, P.O. Box 684, Lake Hopatcong, NJ 07849;
  973-663-0200. Open year-round.
INFORMATION: Lake Hopatcong, Lake Hopatcong State Park,
  P.O. Box 8519, Landing, NJ 07850; 973-398-7010
  Lake Musconetcong, New Jersey Division of Fish and
  Wildlife, Northern Region Office, 26 Route 173 West,
  Hampton, NJ 08827; 973-383-0918
HABITAT TYPE: both lakes have shore development, usually in
  wooded settings, though Lake Musconetcong is less developed
EXPECT TO SEE: eagles, hawks
TAKE NOTE: motorboat traffic is extremely heavy on weekends
  in summer; winds

GETTING THERE

To Lake Hopatcong: Drive north for 1.2 miles on Route 631 (Landing Road) from Exit 28 off I-80. At the junction of Routes 631 and 607, Route 631 turns left. Stay right and drive 0.4 mile north on Route 607. The park entrance will be on the right. This state park is so popular that signs leading to it are everywhere—if you miss them, see your optometrist.

To Lee County Park: Take Exit 30 (Mount Arlington) off I-80 and drive north for 3.6 miles on Route 615 (Howard Boulevard) to the entrance of Lee

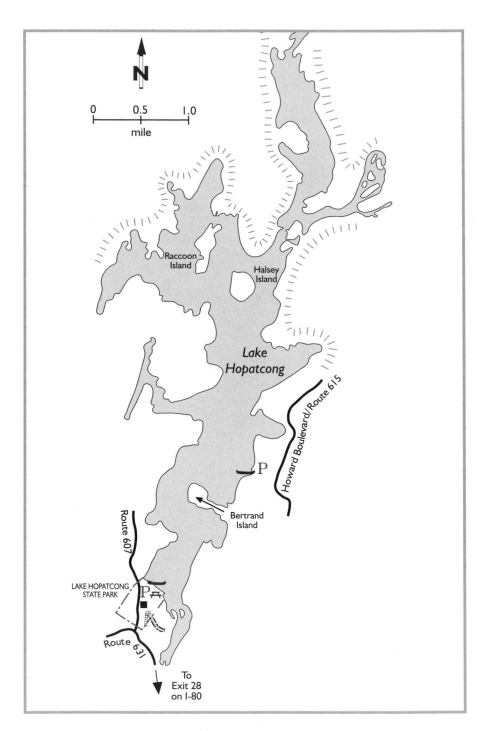

Lake Hopatcong

County Park on the left. Pay the inexpensive launch fee at the booth on the dock to the left.

To Lake Musconetcong: If you're going to Lake Musconetcong because Lake Hopatcong State Park is filled, drive 0.4 mile south on Route 607 from the park entrance, turn right onto Route 631 south (Center Street), and drive 1.6 miles. To the right of the large Welcome to Netcong sign between the road and the lake, a long parking area parallels the road. Pull into the parking area and launch from the south end, where a clearing to the lake is provided.

Lake Hopatcong is the largest natural lake in the state, covering 2,685 acres and more than 40 miles of shoreline. Is it pretty? Well, it's definitely very impressive. There are some charming spots, but houses and marinas pack the shoreline for most of its length. On weekends in summer, it's a veritable zoo, with fishing tournaments, sailing regattas, and the like. I understand from locals that during the week, even in August, it's pretty quiet on the water. There is no limit on the size of gas motors, hence the waters can churn up wildly from boats on weekends. At some point you should paddle it, preferably during the week, just to feel and absorb its expansiveness and to imagine how breathtaking it was for the Native Americans who looked down on the waters from the surrounding hillsides. The name *Hopatcong* is derived from

You have to try Lake Hopatcong at least once, but paddle the waters midweek unless you enjoy wakes from motorboats.

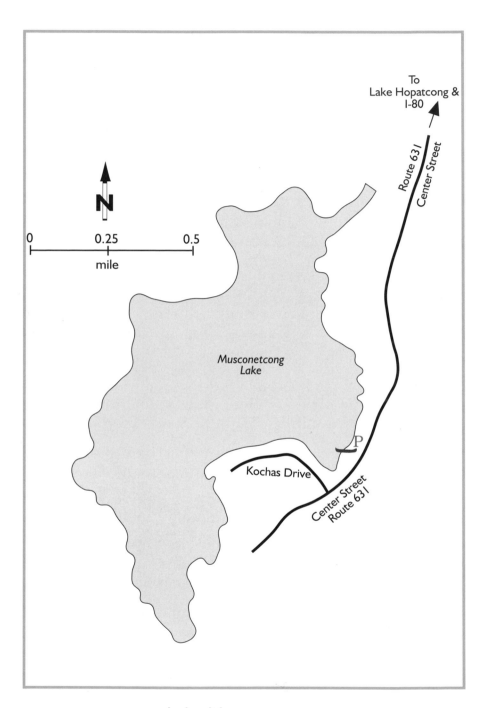

Lake Musconetcong

the Lenni-Lenape Indian word *huppakong*, meaning "honey waters of many coves."

Great for fishing, Lake Hopatcong boasts rainbow and brown trout, hybrid bass, crappie, walleye, pickerel, largemouth and smallmouth bass, perch, sunfish, and other species. Supposedly, the coves are prime habitat for bass. A glacial lake left by the last ice age, its waters are now refurbished by winter snows, and they're cold even in summer. Be adequately prepared with additional clothing when you paddle here. Public access to the lake is provided through Lake Hopatcong State Park on Route 631 on the southwest end of the lake. A public beach is next to the concrete

An early morning mist rises from Lake Musconetcong.

boat ramp; restroom facilities are near the entrance booth. A small entrance fee is charged during summer.

An alternate public access to the lake is through Lee County Park, a third of the way up the lake on the eastern side. A small fee is charged to launch your boat, even in the off-season. Since the extreme northern end of the lake is more scenic and slightly less populated, launching from here puts you a few miles closer.

Lake Musconetcong (a Native American word for "rapidly running river") is only a short drive away from the southern end of Lake Hopatcong. Though it's much smaller at only 329 acres, I preferred this lake and found it more scenic and relaxing. A state park of the same name provides a narrow border of woods around the entire lake in the little town of Netcong.

Silver Lake
Franklin (Sussex)

MAPS: New Jersey Atlas & Gazetteer, Map 19
  USGS Quadrangle, Franklin

AREA: 21 acres

CAMPING: Beaver Hill Campground in Sussex is about 16.0 miles
away. From Route 23, drive south for 1.0 mile on I-94, turn
right, and drive west for 2.0 miles on Route 661 (Beaver Run
Road). Turn left onto Big Spring Road and continue for 0.5
mile. The campground will be on the left. Beaver Hill Campground, P.O. Box 353, Sussex, NJ 07461; 973-827-0670.

INFORMATION: New Jersey Division of Fish and Wildlife,
Northern Region Office, 26 Route 173 West, Hampton, NJ
08827; 973-383-0918

HABITAT TYPE: woods

EXPECT TO SEE: waterfowl

TAKE NOTE: electric outboards only

GETTING THERE

From Route 631 (Franklin Avenue), drive south for 3.0 miles on Route 23
and turn left onto Silver Grove Road. A small bridge crosses over a railroad
track immediately after you turn. Silver Grove Road forks 0.1 mile past the
railroad tracks. Take the left fork, which will be Silver Lake Road, and drive
0.2 mile to the small sign for Silver Lake. From the sign, the rickety road
becomes very narrow, more one-lane than two-lane, so drive the next 1.4 miles
carefully. Turn right at the New Jersey Fish and Game sign and continue for
another 400 feet to the casual launch site and parking area.

It isn't big, but Silver Lake is charming and relaxing. Part of a New
Jersey Fish and Game area, this cozy lake of approximately 20 acres is
located on the outskirts of Fawn Lake, a quiet little community adjacent
to Hamburg Mountain Wildlife Management Area. Densely forested
game lands encircle the lake, and a small, shrub-covered rocky island

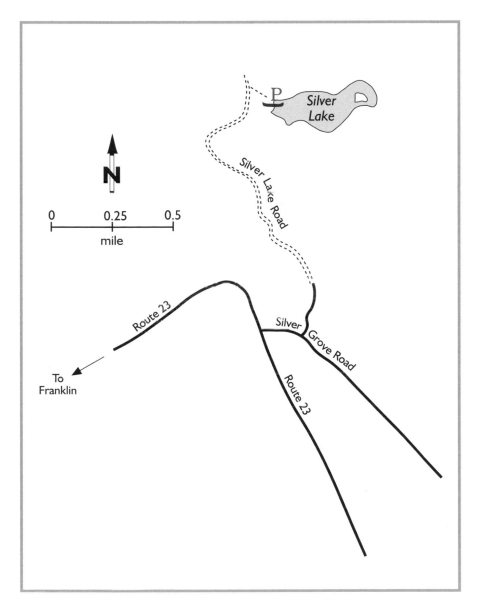

Silver Lake

on the south end provides a great picnic spot in a tranquil setting. This isn't a place where you can spend an entire afternoon exploring, yet you could easily pass an hour or more observing and photographing the abundant birdlife as you paddle slowly around the lake. If you're lucky, you might spot a raccoon. I saw several sets of tracks around the sandy

Solitude is what you'll find at this quaint little lake near Hamburg Mountain.

launch site, and several deer trails led into the lake. Only electric outboards are allowed, guaranteeing a quiet paddle.

If you're in the area, complete the day with visits to the famous Franklin Mines, Franklin Museum, and several gem shops in the nearby town of Franklin. Rocks in this region of New Jersey have gone through dramatic geologic changes as the plates below the earth's crust collided over millions of years to form the Appalachian Mountains. This process resulted in the formation of more than a hundred different minerals, many of which have not been discovered anywhere else in the world. Franklinite, a black, zinc-iron oxide mineral, was named for the town and has been found only in Franklin and the neighboring town of Ogdensburg.

Mine tours make a great adventure for children, who put on a miner's helmet and walk through tunnels while a guide talks about mining operations and the various minerals found there. In the gem shops, children usually go right for pyrite, a heavy mineral known as "fool's gold" because of its glistening resemblance in color and weight to the real thing.

~ 16 ~

Cranberry Lake
Cranberry Lake (Sussex)

MAPS: New Jersey Atlas & Gazetteer, Map 24
  USGS Quadrangle, Stanhope
AREA: 179 acres
INFORMATION: New Jersey Division of Fish and Wildlife,
  Northern Region Office, 26 Route 173 West, Hampton, NJ
  08827; 973-383-0918
HABITAT TYPE: dense woodland on the southern half; lake
  development
EXPECT TO SEE: hawks, eagles
TAKE NOTE: motorboats

GETTING THERE

From Route 607, drive 3.2 miles north on Route 206, turn left onto South Shore Road, and drive 0.2 mile. A Cranberry Lake Park sign will be on the right. The right turn onto the gravel road is a very sharp hairpin turn that goes up a short but steep embankment. At the top of the embankment, turn right. Limited parking is immediately to the right. The concrete boat launch is down the road about 150 feet. You don't need to use the ramp if you can portage your kayak over the small guardrail and across the narrow dirt and stone dike to the water.

The 179-acre Cranberry Lake is almost cut in half by a long, narrow peninsula barely attached on its western side, creating more shoreline to explore. Cranberry Lake Park on the northeast corner of the lake provides a boat launch, limited parking, and a hiking trail that travels along the stone dike edging the lake's southeastern shore. While you're there, examine the boulders that line the parking area for black, oblong hornblende crystals. Look for the shiny, sheetlike mineral black muscovite, which appears to have an oily sheen over its surface.

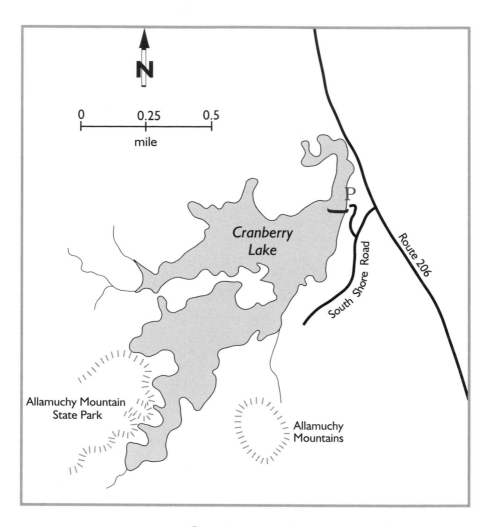

Cranberry Lake

Saving the best for last, start your trip to the right (north) of the launch and paddle around the northern half of the lake. Once you're around the peninsula on the western side, you'll find the most remote and prettiest paddling as you enter the southern half of the lake, where mountains rise sharply. Allamuchy Mountain State Park grips the southern end of Cranberry Lake with tenacious fingers, cradling quiet coves that beg you to stop paddling, close your eyes, and breathe in the fresh mountain air of this tranquil hideaway.

Muskrat

Semiaquatic rodents, muskrats live in and around lakes, ponds, fresh- and saltwater marshes, and slow-moving streams throughout North America. Their common name is derived from the musk glands predominant beneath the skin on the lower abdomen of males, which produce a strong scent. Averaging 2 feet in length, the muskrat's dark gray or brown fur fools many people into thinking they've spotted a beaver. A muskrat's partially webbed hind feet act as paddles, and its long, scaly, hairless tail, flattened sideways, acts as a rudder in the water. Mainly nocturnal, they're most visible at dawn or dusk, when they leave their burrows to feed on aquatic plants. Although primarily vegetarians preferring cattails, arrowhead weed, pond-weed, bulbs, and tubers, they will occasionally dine on snails, crayfish, frogs, and carrion when plants are scarce. Muskrats clean all their food, washing it before consumption.

In marshlands, muskrats build dome-shaped houses as large as 6 to 8 feet across and 2 feet high using reeds, *Phragmites,* and mud. Check channel corners as you paddle by for chewed-off reeds, the telltale sign that a muskrat lives nearby—probably within 150 feet. Houses are located near the water, where an extensive tunnel system leads to several underwater entrances. In tidal waters, lakes, and slow-moving streams with steep banks they will sometimes make their homes by burrowing into the bank, and a small dome is built only for a surface entrance. Reeds and grasses line the main room above the high-water line. Muskrats construct special food huts near the main hut to store vegetative roots and grasses to use while nursing or during bad weather.

Breeding takes place from late March through July, producing an average of four litters of five to seven young each year. Although muskrats do not mate for life, they are thought to have only one mate during rearing seasons. Gestation lasts about a month, and babies are weaned by two months of age. As self-regulating animals, their population density, habitat quality, and food availability all affect the number and size of litters in a given year. Usually a solitary animal, except when mating, muskrats often share a communal den during winter. They are prey for foxes, hawks, raccoons, coyotes, and owls.

Large populations of muskrats can be deleterious to the aquatic vegetation necessary for other wildlife, and their burrowing activities weaken dikes and earthen dams. On the commercial scale, muskrats are valued for their fur and are often referred to as "river mink."

Central New Jersey

Northwest of an imaginary line running approximately from Trenton on the Delaware River, to New Brunswick on the Atlantic Ocean, start the rolling hills of the Piedmont Plateau, which grade into the higher mountains of northwestern New Jersey. Southeast of this line, the rolling hills gently flatten into a low coastal plain. Barrier islands rim the Atlantic Ocean like a necklace and help protect developed coastal areas from pounding ocean waves. The gravel and sand of the coastal plain gradually become dirt rich with minerals, on which horse and agricultural farms flourish. Valleys become natural holding basins for rainwater and small streams. Slightly cooler weather in the hills creates the southern extent of northern birds, such as the bobolink, which rarely make it south of Trenton during summer.

The Delaware and Raritan Canal connects the Delaware River with the Raritan River, which flows into Raritan Bay on the Atlantic Ocean. This historic route once provided essential passage for the transportation of coal and other cargo from Pennsylvania to New York City and other towns along the eastern seaboard between 1834 and 1932. Mules plodded along the towpath beside the canal, pulling barges laden with goods on a two-day journey from Bordentown to New Brunswick. Many historically designated bridge-tenders' houses and hand-laid cobblestone spillways along the canal offer a glimpse of the era before railroads replaced water as an economic and efficient mode of transportation. The canal and towpath are now part of the National Recreational Trail System.

～ 17 ～

Delaware and Raritan Canal
South Bound Brook to Griggstown (Sussex)

MAPS: New Jersey Atlas & Gazetteer, Maps 36 and 37
USGS Quadrangles, Bound Brook and Monmouth Junction

LENGTH: the canal length between lock portages varies from 3 to 10 miles

INFORMATION: Delaware & Raritan Canal Park, 625 Canal Road, Somerset, NJ 08873; 732-873-3050

HABITAT TYPE: open woods with some fields; limited shore development

EXPECT TO SEE: waterfowl

TAKE NOTE: Should you choose to portage the locks instead of making a round trip, be aware that the average portage length is 0.25 mile. Other than the length, portages are easy—the terrain is level. Avoid the canal that parallels the Delaware River, because the current runs too swiftly for a two-way trip and can even be dangerous in times of high water. You could store your bike at a lock farther south, but the nonstop traffic along Route 29 offsets some of the aesthetics of paddling between the quaint towns of Lambertville, Stockton, and Washington's Crossing. If you choose to paddle it, be prepared to go elsewhere if the water is too turbulent.

GETTING THERE

Numerous designated parking lots with boat access are found next to the towpath along the canal. I have listed only a few, chosen for their historic settings and scenic waters.

To access the canal at Amwell and Blackwells Mills from Route 206, drive east for 3.6 miles on Route 514 (Amwell Road). After passing over the Millstone River, look for the parking lot on the left, on the west side of the canal in Amwell. Launch directly into the canal from there. You can paddle north for 3.2 miles before encountering a lock. To get to Blackwells Mills, continue on Route 514 across the canal, turn right onto Canal Road, and drive for 2.2 miles to Blackwells Mills Road. Turn right and cross over the canal. Launch from the west side of the canal, and leave your car in the large

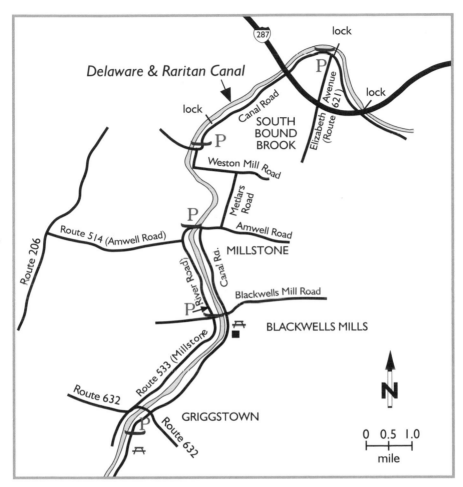

Delaware and Raritan Canal

parking lot on the left, about 100 feet down the hill from the canal. Other launch locations are depicted on the map.

The park office is located at Blackwells Mills. From Route 514, drive south for 2.1 miles on Route 533 (Millstone River Road). Turn left onto Blackwells Mills Road and drive for 0.2 mile. Turn right onto Canal Road and drive about 100 feet to the office on the left.

Ask anyone who paddles the Delaware and Raritan Canal, and they'll tell you they think it more a narrow lake than a river. Overflow culverts drain excessive water from the canal into nearby waterways such as the

Raritan and Millstone Rivers, thus retaining a slow flow rate through-out the canal's length. In times of insufficient rain, water is pumped into the canal from these same nearby rivers. The original canal, which ran from Bordentown to New Brunswick, was 44 miles long and 70 feet wide. A 13-mile feeder canal, which provided water for the current, ran from Bull's Island on the Delaware River above Raven Rock to Trenton. Today approximately 36 miles of the original canal remain intact, along with 12 miles of the feeder canal. Around 70 million gallons of water per day from this system supplement the water supply of many communities in central New Jersey. The Green Acres Program has efforts under way to widen the current Delaware & Raritan Canal Park, which narrowly rims 70 miles of the main canal and feeder.

Quaint villages such as Griggstown and Blackwells Mills have retained their nineteenth-century architecture, transporting you back in time as you glide past historic houses and under turn-of-the-century bridges. Joggers, bikers, and strollers enjoy the earthen towpath that parallels the canal as it winds its way past miles of fields and forests between towns. Trees burst with color in autumn when maple, sycamore, beech, and hickory display their finery before the onset of winter. You may have to duck a bit when passing under one or more of

The towpath on the left runs alongside the canal, providing an opportunity to bike or jog before or after your paddle.

the old, low bridges that span the canal. Paddling up and back the waterway is easy, but this also would be the perfect opportunity to combine paddling with biking or hiking.

Griggstown is one of the more historic villages along the route and features a wooden canal bridge, Mule Tender's Barracks Canal Museum, a bridge-tender's house and station, and an old mill site. Large, grassy fields with picnic tables and grills are within a short walking distance of the canal access. Spend the morning paddling the canal, have a picnic lunch, then visit the bridge-tender's house in the afternoon to get a glimpse into the world of those who once lived here. Canoes can be rented in Griggstown from private concessionaires.

Along Blackwells Mills, another charming village, you'll find a bridge-tender's house, a rickety wooden bridge, and an old mill site along the canal. Picnic tables and grills are located around a large field with views of the river.

18

Lake Surprise
Mountainside (Union)

MAPS: New Jersey Atlas & Gazetteer, Map 31
USGS Quadrangle, Roselle
AREA: 25 acres
INFORMATION: Trailside Nature and Science Center, 452 New Providence Road, Mountainside, NJ 07092; 908-789-3670
HABITAT TYPE: woods and bogs
EXPECT TO SEE: waterfowl

GETTING THERE

From Route 22, take the Watchung Reservation/Summit Road exit near the town of Mountainside. Drive 1.2 miles west on Summit Road, turn left onto Summit Lane, and drive for 0.8 mile. At the circle, make the first right—there will be a sign pointing toward the lake. Stay to the right on the main road for 1.2 miles to the lake. Launch from the east side of the bridge (as you approach the lake) and park in the lot on the west side of the bridge 50 feet up the road.

The aptly named Lake Surprise, a quaint 25-acre lake, was a surprise to find in the midst of heavily populated towns. Located in a ravine within the 2,000-acre Watchung Reservation, the lake is surrounded by hemlock and pine interspersed with beech, maple, locust, and other hardwoods. The reservation hosts numerous activities, including horseback riding, hiking, an environmental activity center, a butterfly garden, picnic groves, and a planetarium.

At 1.0 mile long and 100 feet wide, the lake will not provide a long paddle, but the setting is gorgeous—perfect for a quick trip at the end of a hectic day and ideal for the novice. Its depth averages 4 feet, with a number of spots on the southwest end reaching 8 feet. Painted and spotted turtles, butterflies, and birds are its main wildlife. Miles of hiking trails take you up and down mountainous terrain, where you're likely to encounter deer, foxes, and skunks.

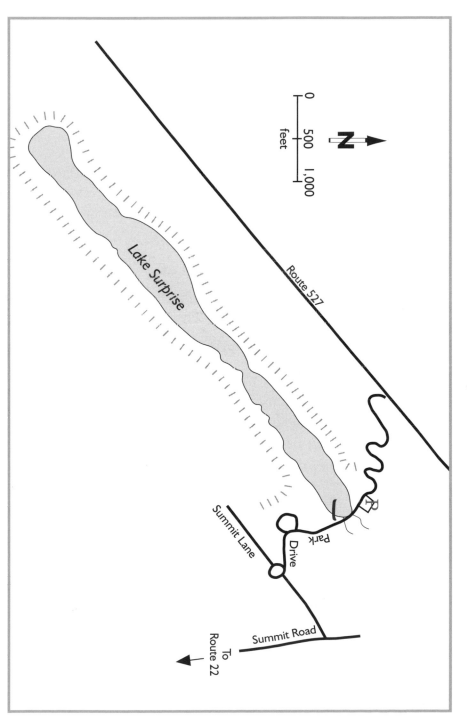

Lake Surprise

19

Lakes Carasaljo and Shenandoah
Lakewood (Ocean)

MAPS: New Jersey Atlas & Gazetteer, Map 50
USGS Quadrangle, Lakewood

AREA: Lake Carasaljo, 67 acres
Lake Shenandoah, 50 acres

INFORMATION: New Jersey Division of Fish and Wildlife, Central
Region (Assunpink WMA), 386 Clarksburg–Robbinsville
Road, Robbinsville, NJ 08691; 609-259-2132

HABITAT TYPE: Lake Carasaljo—woods and marshes, with shore
development; Lake Shenandoah—woods and marshes

EXPECT TO SEE: waterfowl, wading birds, marsh plants

TAKE NOTE: electric motorboats are permitted on Lake
Shenandoah only

GETTING THERE

To Lake Carasaljo: From the south, drive north on Route 9 from Route 70. At
the Route 628 junction, continue north for 0.7 mile on Route 9 to Central
Avenue. Turn left onto Central Avenue and make an immediate right onto
South Lake Drive. Drive for 0.9 mile to the stone launch site and parking
area on the right.

From the north, take Route 9 south to Main Street in Lakewood—a sign
for Route 528 east is on the left. Continue south on Route 9 for two blocks,
passing the lake on the right, and turn right onto Central Avenue. Continue
as above.

To Lake Shenandoah: From Route 9, drive east for 1.0 mile on Route 528
(Cedar Bridge Avenue), turn left onto South Clover Street, and drive for
0.5 mile to the park entrance on the right. The boat ramp and parking area are
right inside the entrance.

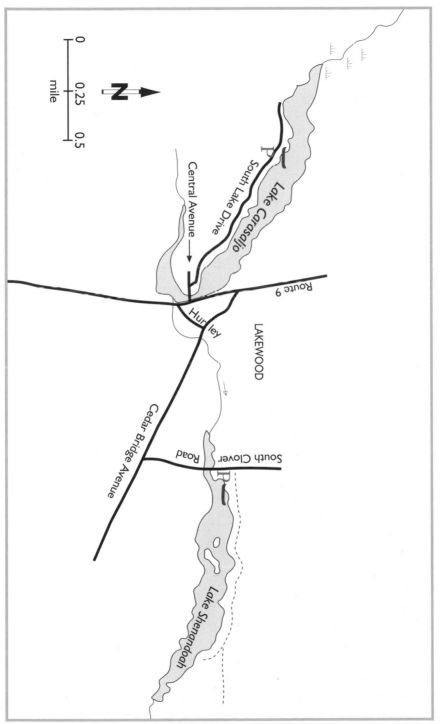

Lakes Carasaljo and Shenandoah

An island adds adventure when you paddle Lake Shenandoah.

It was a pleasure to find two nice lakes to paddle in a densely populated town rife with industrial parks. Long and narrow, Lake Carasaljo's 67-acre expanse is bordered almost completely by a wide, lightly wooded swath of municipal park. Bikers, joggers, and walkers make their way along a trail on the southern shore that weaves through the trees along the shoreline. A small, sandy swimming beach is located midway on the north side. The best paddling is on the western half, away from Route 9. Depending on water levels, you may be able to paddle up the Carasaljo River at the extreme western end of the lake for 0.5 mile or more.

Lake Shenandoah County Park was once part of John D. Rockefeller's vacation estate, to which hemlock and unique specimen trees were imported from all over the country. More than 140 acres of park offer biking and hiking trails, a small picnic area, and restrooms. Dense woods to the south, east, and northeast surround the park's 50-acre lake. On the northwest side, tall grasses give way to dense shrubs and saplings, a perfect habitat for box turtles and black racers, a fast-moving, satiny black snake. Two islands halfway down the lake add a spark of interest to your trip. Though Lake Shenandoah may be a little smaller, its location on the outskirts of town makes this a more scenic paddle.

Osprey

For years the osprey population suffered declines, due in large part to pesticides and habitat destruction. With the help of artificial nesting sites and a ban on DDT, they are making a tremendous comeback. Also known as fish hawks, they are the only bird of prey (raptor) whose front talons turn backward and the only one that plunges feetfirst into the water. Spines on the osprey's toes enable it to hold on to slippery fish, its main prey. These birds are known to hunt the occasional small rodent or crustacean when fishing is poor.

The osprey favors open streams, rivers, and lakes, nesting in treetops near water. Brown above and white below, its most distinguishing field marks are its broad, black cheek patch and black wrist patches. The adult wingspan of an osprey averages 4 to 4.5 feet, and males are slightly smaller in size than females.

Females choose partners based on nest location, and the pair generally mate for life. Both adults help build the large stick nest, which measures 3 to

5 feet in diameter. While males and females may winter in different locations, they return to their nest within a few days of each other. Ospreys arrive in southern New Jersey around the end of March and in northern New Jersey a week or two later. Courtship flights, a graceful touch-and-go aerial maneuver, can be seen the first week or two after their arrival as mating pairs are made or renewed. Part of the mating ritual entails the male catching fish for the female, to prove that he will be, or still is, a good provider.

From pairing until egg laying, females are fed by the males. Both adults assist in repairing the old nest, shoring up walls with fresh twigs and lining the bottom with mucky sod. From my personal observations, both will bring in twigs but more often than not the female does the arranging.

When not hunting, the male can be found on his roost about 100 yards away and within visual contact of the nest. At the first hint of danger, such as human intrusion or blackbird mobbing, the female emits a high-pitched *eep, eep, eep* sound, a signal for the male to come flying to the rescue. As the female nears egg-laying time, she stays closer to the nest, leaving infrequently to stretch her wings. Once the eggs (two to four) are laid, she hunkers down in the nest, with only the top of her head visible to a careful observer. The female incubates the eggs and will trade off periodically with the male. After catching a fish, the male eats the head and neck area, then brings the remainder to the nest and takes over incubation while the female feeds. After the female has eaten and preened, she resumes incubation and the male returns to his proximal roost.

Their young hatch about five weeks after the eggs are laid, but it will take an additional seven to eight weeks before they are ready to leave the nest. Even then, the parents must provide food for the first few weeks until the young can hunt well enough on their own. Catching fish through the warped air–water interface evidently requires practice, practice, and more practice. By mid-October, ospreys start heading south to their favorite wintering ground.

～20～
Manasquan Reservoir
Farmingdale (Monmouth)

MAPS: New Jersey Atlas & Gazetteer, Map 50
USGS Quadrangle, Farmingdale

AREA: 720 acres

CAMPING: The Pine Cone Campground is nearby in Freehold Acres. From the junction of Routes 33 and 9, drive 5.5 miles south on Route 9, then go 1.5 miles west on West Farms Road. Pine Cone Campground, P.O. Box 7047, Department N, Freehold, N.J. 07728; 732-462-2230.

INFORMATION: New Jersey Division of Fish and Wildlife, Central Region (Assunpink WMA), 386 Clarksburg-Robbinsville Road, Robbinsville, NJ 08691; 609-259-2132

HABITAT TYPE: open

EXPECT TO SEE: waterfowl

TAKE NOTE: electric motorboats only; winds

GETTING THERE

From Route 9 at its junction with I-195, drive north for 0.2 mile on Route 9. Turn right onto Georgia Tavern Road and drive for 0.4 mile, then turn right onto Windeler Road (there is a sign for Manasquan Reservoir at Windeler Road). Drive 2.0 miles to the park entrance on the left and follow signs to the boat launch. There is a nominal boat ramp fee year-round and a park entrance fee in summer.

The 720-acre Manasquan Reservoir will keep you paddling for hours. Outboard and canoe rentals are available on the lower level of the visitor center next to the boat ramp. The upper level of the visitor center houses a food concession, operated only during summer months, as well as environmental displays and an observation deck. Horseback riding is available, and a jogging and biking path extends around the reservoir's perimeter. Numerous hiking trails meander through the woods.

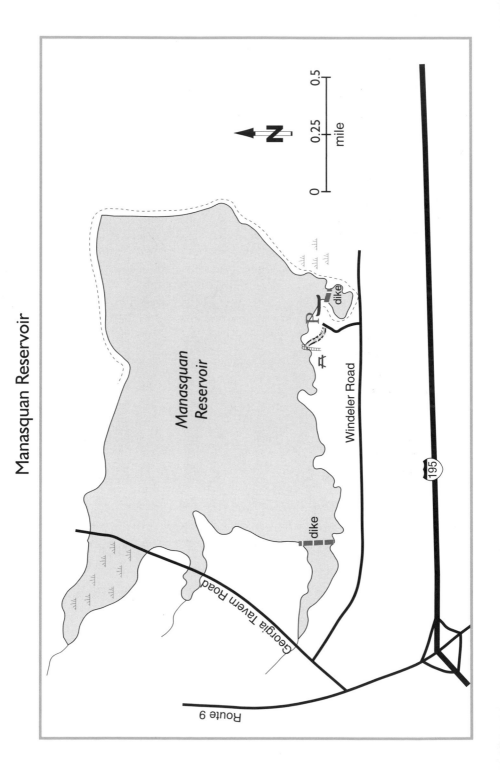

Manasquan Reservoir

Dainty asters sprinkle the lakeside in late summer.

Turn right from the launch to paddle past a cove filled with dead trees bleached silvery gray from the sun. Woodpeckers occasionally tap their way into the hollow core of the taller dead trees in early summer. Reportedly, fishing is excellent, particularly for crappies, bass, and trout.

Prospertown Lake
Prospertown (Ocean)

MAPS: New Jersey Atlas & Gazetteer, Map 49
  USGS Quadrangle, Roosevelt

AREA: 80 acres

CAMPING: The Timberland Lake Campground is nearby. From
  Prospertown Lake, drive south on Route 537 for 0.75 mile.
  Turn left onto Hawkin Road. Go 0.25 mile and turn left onto
  Reed Road. Timberland Lake Campground, P.O. Box 48,
  Jackson, NJ, 08527; 732-928-0500.

INFORMATION: New Jersey Division of Fish and Wildlife, Central
  Region (Assunpink WMA), 386 Clarksburg–Robbinsville
  Road, Robbinsville, NJ 08691; 609-259-2132

HABITAT TYPE: woods

EXPECT TO SEE: waterfowl, hawks, deer, turtles

TAKE NOTE: no motors are allowed, though some may sneak in

GETTING THERE

Prospertown Lake is conveniently located just off Route 537, approximately
2.6 miles south of Exit 16 off I-195. Millers Mill Road is exactly at Mile
Marker 39 on the west side of Route 537. The entrance to the lake is about
200 feet south of Mile Marker 39 on the left. A sign designating the entrance
to the lake is clearly visible.

Hours of paddling can be enjoyed in this remote yet easily accessible
location surrounded by Prospertown Wildlife Management Area. Neither gas nor electric motors are permitted, but since the lake is not
patrolled regularly, a few tend to slip in now and then. Nevertheless,
these waters rarely become crowded, even on the hottest summer
weekend. A narrow stretch of open sandy beach near the launch can get
a bit busy at dusk, when local anglers come try their luck for an hour
or two. If you paddle toward the extreme northeast end, you'll find

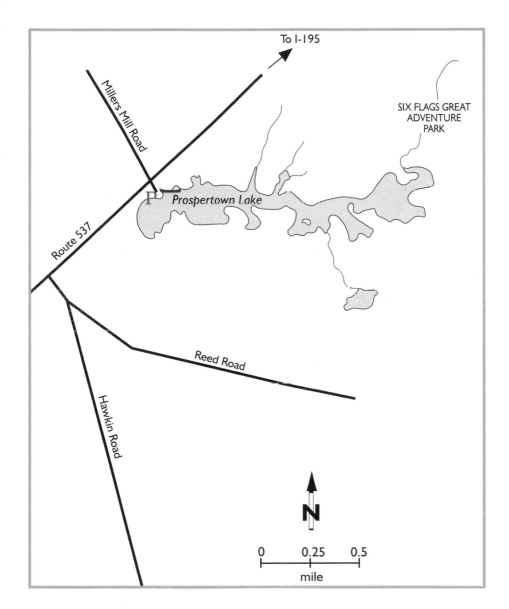

To I-195

Millers Mill Road

SIX FLAGS GREAT
ADVENTURE
PARK

Prospertown Lake

Route 537

Reed Road

Hawkin Road

N

| 0 | 0.25 | 0.5 |
mile

Prospertown Lake

yourself entering grounds owned by Six Flags Great Adventure Park.
No, you won't be permitted to land on their property; guards continually
patrol this section. Though located near this popular attraction, traffic
on Route 537 by the lake is minimal in this sparsely populated area of
the state.

The sandy beach area along one edge of the lake is a wonderful spot to picnic.

A few small islands break up the lake's surface close to shore by the bend in the northeast section. Inlets and coves of all sizes provide excellent habitat for turtles, deer, raccoons, beavers, and waterfowl. Painted and spotted turtles are a common sight on sunny shores and logs, while low grasses around the launch site harbor garter snakes. Around the bend to the northeast, a picturesque area of silvery-smooth dead trees provides a prime habitat for woodpeckers. Hawks and vultures frequent the skies above the lake, while blue jays and songbirds delight in the pristine habitat of dense beech, hickory, and hardwood forests.

The water depth in this 80-acre lake extends to about 21 feet; the deeper portions are found closer to the side opposite the launch. Bass, catfish, sunfish, and crappies are the most sought-after species by anglers.

～ 22 ～

Assunpink, Stone Tavern, and Rising Sun Lakes
Roosevelt (Monmouth)

MAPS: New Jersey Atlas & Gazetteer, Map 43
USGS Quadrangles, Allentown and Roosevelt

AREA: Assunpink Lake, 225 acres
Stone Tavern Lake, 52 acres
Rising Sun Lake, 38 acres

INFORMATION: New Jersey Division of Fish and Wildlife, Central
Region (Assunpink WMA), 386 Clarksburg–Robbinsville
Road, Robbinsville, NJ 08691; 609-259-2132

HABITAT TYPE: woods and marshes

EXPECT TO SEE: turtles, hawks, eagles, waterfowl

TAKE NOTE: electric motorboats only on all three lakes

GETTING THERE

To Lake Assunpink: Take I-195 to Exit 11 (Hightstown/Imlaystown). Drive
north for 2.6 miles toward Hightstown on Imlaystown–Hightstown Road
to the T, turn left, and drive 100 feet to the huge parking and launch area.
The road becomes sand for the last 1.3 miles after crossing Herbert/East
Branch Road.

To Stone Tavern Lake: From Imlaystown–Hightstown Road, drive 1.8
miles east on East Branch Road (it will make a right bend 0.5 mile into the
drive). You will pass a narrow dirt road on the left (north) about 150 feet
before the gray-stone entrance road, also on the left. Drive 0.4 mile to the
lake; there is parking for about ten cars and a launch from the sandy beach.

To Rising Sun Lake: From Imlaystown–Hightstown Road just north of
I-195, drive 3.2 miles east on Route 524 (New Canton–Stone Tavern Road).
Turn left (north) onto Route 571 (Rising Sun Tavern Road) and drive 1.3 miles
to the dirt entrance road on the left (west). Parking and the dirt launch are
about 200 feet ahead.

Assunpink, Stone Tavern, and Rising Sun Lakes

Far from civilization, Stone Tavern Lake invites you to paddle its tranquil waters.

Get out here and paddle! More than 5,000 acres of wildlife management area surround three beautiful lakes: 225-acre Lake Assunpink, 52-acre Stone Tavern Lake, and 38-acre Rising Sun Lake. Each has its own character, its own special charm. With its large size and numerous coves and inlets, Lake Assunpink offers more hours of paddling pleasure. Although it's never very crowded, anglers frequent this lake on summer weekends looking for bass and pickerel. Sweetgum, pine, red maple, and oak dominate the surrounding woods behind a screen of cattails, *Phragmites*, mulberry bushes, and joe-pye weed bordering the water.

Joe-pye weed *(Eupatorium maculatum)* was used extensively by Native Americans to cure renal problems, especially kidney stones. Reputed Native American healer Joe Pye lived in colonial New England and used this herb to cure typhoid and other fevers. During late summer, the plant develops purplish brown clusters of flowers that add a soft touch of color to swampy borders.

Stone Tavern Lake is smaller but more nestled in the woods and very tranquil. Cast your eyes skyward occasionally to spot one of the many red-tailed hawks that frequent the area as you explore the lake's numerous coves. Wild blueberry and fragrant sweet pepperbush nudge their way into the dappled sunlight. Rising Sun Lake, the smallest of the three, sits among woods and open fields. Only electric motors are permitted on the lakes, assuring a quiet paddle.

Forge Pond
Brick (Ocean)

MAPS: New Jersey Atlas & Gazetteer, Map 50
  USGS Quadrangle, Lakewood
AREA: 45 acres
HABITAT TYPE: open woods and marshes
EXPECT TO SEE: waterfowl, shore birds, wading birds
TAKE NOTE: electric motorboats only

GETTING THERE

At the horrendous junction of Routes 88 and 70, take Route 70 East and drive for 0.3 mile to the entrance, which is beside a small strip mall. Parking is available for about ten cars.

Forty-five acres are yours to enjoy in the midst of this bustling city. During the day, egrets, blue herons, songbirds, box and painted turtles, and huge snapping turtles are plentiful. An occasional water snake may be spotted slithering along the surface. The serene pond area is historically where the Lenni-Lenape Indians met and performed their rituals, spring through fall. From the pond you can paddle under the Route 70 bridge and onto the Metedeconk River. There is a mild tidal current as Forge Pond flows into Barnegat Bay, about 3.5 miles down the narrow river. The river is surrounded for a short distance by a wildlife area to the south and a residential shore to the north, where it widens and becomes choppier. Only electric outboards are permitted on the pond, but if you enter the Metedeconk River, anything goes.

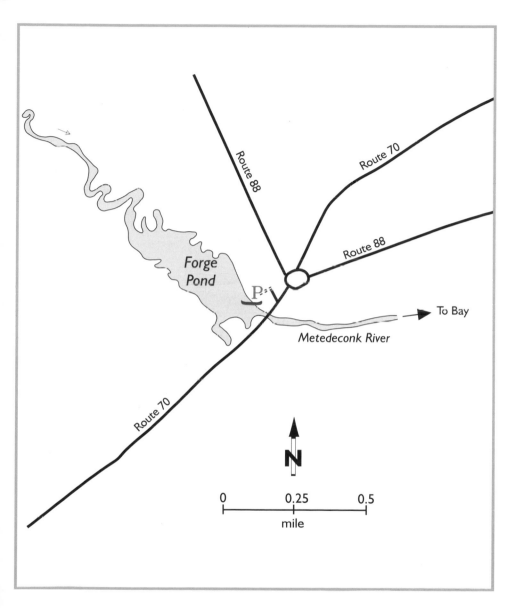

Forge Pond

～24～

Shadow Lake
Red Bank (Monmouth)

MAPS: New Jersey Atlas & Gazetteer, Map 44
USGS Quadrangle, Long Branch
AREA: 88 acres
INFORMATION: New Jersey Division of Fish and Wildlife, Central
Region (Assunpink WMA), 386 Clarksburg–Robbinsville
Road, Robbinsville, NJ 08691; 609-259-2132
HABITAT TYPE: woods
EXPECT TO SEE: waterfowl, deer, raccoons
TAKE NOTE: a dam at the eastern end is well marked

GETTING THERE

From Southbound Garden State Parkway: Take Exit 109, turn left at the end of the ramp, and drive 0.3 mile east on Route 520 (Newman Springs Road). Turn left onto Half Mile Road and drive for 0.6 mile. Turn left onto West Front Street and continue for 0.5 mile. A sign is on the right for Stevenson Park. Turn right into the park (Shady Oak Way) and drive for 0.2 mile. Turn right immediately past the small bridge over the creek onto the dirt road. The launch site is about 100 feet down on the right.

From Northbound Garden State Parkway: Take Exit 109. As you come down the exit ramp, stay left, watching for signs for Half Mile Road, which will be straight ahead of you at the bottom of the ramp. Cross Route 520 onto Half Mile Road and proceed as above.

It is like a fairy tale. Tucked away neatly at the bottom of a steep hill in Stevenson Park, the dirt launch at Shadow Lake faces thickly wooded, steep hills surrounding its western half. Though half of the northern shore and part of the southern are privately owned, you'd never guess it, because most of the houses sit near the top of steep hills deep within the thick woods. Only when you get close to the dam on the lake's eastern end will civilization become more visible. A

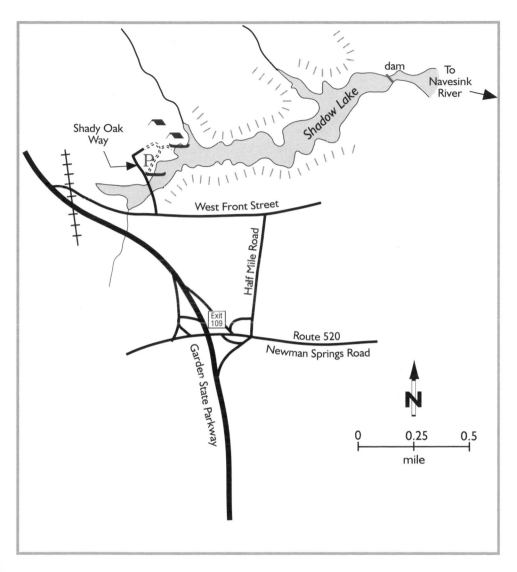

Shadow Lake

dirt road leads off from the park down a winding passage to the lake, where underbrush has been cleared in a small area to accommodate a few picnic tables.

Pine, beech, hickory, maple, and ash march up the steep hills overlooking waters inhabited by sunfish, smallmouth and largemouth bass, trout, and pickerel. The depth in this 88-acre lake averages 15 feet, with

Swans glide among a carpet of water lilies in the shallow terminus of Shadow Lake.

depths to more than 30 feet on the eastern end closer to the dam. To the right of the launch, where a stream enters the lake, ducks and geese share a carpet of white and yellow pond lilies with painted turtles and frogs. Part of this small, shallow area is private property and posted prominently as such.

~ 25 ~

Round Valley Reservoir
Lebanon (Hunterdon)

MAPS: New Jersey Atlas & Gazetteer, Map 35
   USGS Quadrangles, High Bridge and Flemington
AREA: 2,350 acres
CAMPING AND INFORMATION: Round Valley Recreation Area,
   Box 45D, Lebanon Stanton Road, Lebanon, NJ 08833;
   908-236-6355
HABITAT TYPE: mostly dense woods; some open areas near
   the entrance
EXPECT TO SEE: hawks, eagles, songbirds
TAKE NOTE: winds; motorboats to 10 HP only

GETTING THERE

From the East: Take I-78 west to Exit 20 toward Lebanon/Round Valley
Recreation Area. It will merge into Route 639 south (Cokesbury Road).
Drive for 0.3 mile to the T at Main Street. Turn left and go 0.1 mile to Route
629 (Cherry Street). Turn right and drive 1.4 miles to the boat launch
entrance road on the left. Park at the boat launch area. If you continue for
another 0.9 mile, you'll find the entrance to the small recreational lake (no
boating) with a beach, picnic grove, and a playground.

   From the West: Take I-78 east to Exit 18 (Lebanon/Route 22 east). Follow Route 22 east for 1.6 miles, veer right onto Main Street, drive 0.6 mile
to Route 629 (Cherry Street), and continue as above. Large signs are posted
all along the roads for a 5.0-mile radius around the reservoir, making it
impossible to miss. A fee is charged in summer.

At 2,350 acres, Round Valley is the state's largest reservoir and its second largest body of fresh water, surpassed only by Lake Hopatcong. It
is also one of the most heavily fished waters in the region. The reservoir opened in 1972 as a backup to nearby Spruce Run, and its shape is
primarily—you guessed it—round. As with Merrill Creek (Trip 13) and

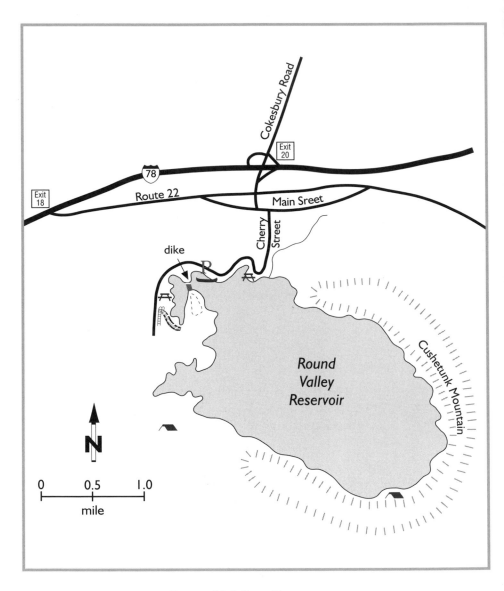

Round Valley Reservoir

Spruce Run (Trip 26), a warning light flashes from a tower when winds reach 25 miles per hour for five seconds or more, requiring all boats to head back to the launch. Other than a concrete dam to the left of the launch, mixed oak-hardwood forests with an occasional thick stand of pines hug the shoreline.

Leaving behind the busy launch area, paddle to the right around the small peninsula, where the waters open wide. Shallow coves and small points of land break up the shoreline for an interesting paddle, but don't forget to check the sky occasionally for bald eagles searching for a meal. Hawks and vultures circle in the thermals of air above the lake; warblers, kingfishers, blue jays, finches, and other songbirds flit in and about the trees along the water.

I paddled the perimeter of the reservoir with two local kayakers who advised hugging the shores on weekends between Independence Day and Labor Day. Evidently, the central waters can become crazed with anglers. One kayaker who paddles here often mentioned that he sees eagles plunge for fish "at least once each summer." Take advantage of camping facilities in the park around the time of a full moon and enjoy relaxing moonlight paddles—but don't forget a waterproof flashlight and an emergency strobe.

A kayaker paddles out to explore the vast waters of Round Valley Reservoir and try his luck at fishing.

Bring fishing equipment along if you'd like, because Round Valley is well known for its excellent sport. Largemouth and smallmouth bass, brown and rainbow trout, yellow and white perch (great panfish), and large sunfish all inhabit the waters, which reach a depth of 175 feet. This is the only lake in New Jersey with a population of reproducing lake trout.

Wilderness family campsites, some accessible only by boat, highlight an extended trip. Miles of hiking and biking trails pass through hemlock valleys and hardwood highlands. The park is open twenty-four hours a day, 365 days a year, and ramp access is free. Boating is prohibited at the recreation lake, which is accessible through the park's main entrance for those who wish to enjoy the beach, playground, and large picnic area.

～26～

Spruce Run Reservoir
Clinton (Hunterdon)

MAPS: New Jersey Atlas & Gazetteer, Map 29
  USGS Quadrangle, High Bridge
AREA: 1,290 acres
CAMPING AND INFORMATION: Spruce Run State Park, 1 Van
  Syckel's Corner Road, Clinton, NJ 08809; 908-638-8572
HABITAT TYPE: woods
EXPECT TO SEE: eagles, hawks, waterfowl, foxes, raccoons
TAKE NOTE: winds; motorboats to 10 HP only

GETTING THERE

Take Exit 12 off I-78 and turn north onto Route 635. Drive for 1.1 miles, turn right onto Van Syckel's Corner Road, and continue for 2.0 miles to the park entrance on the right. A modest fee is charged to enter the main park in summer.

Built in 1965 for the Elizabethtown Water Company, this near-1,300-acre reservoir's highly irregular outline resembles a serpentine monster. You could spend a week paddling in and out of all the little nooks and crannies. In my opinion, this is the most interesting of the three area reservoirs, even though it's only half the size of Round Valley (Trip 25; the third is Merrill Creek Reservoir, Trip 13). Campsites are available on the grounds, inviting you to spend a few rewarding days. Make reservations ahead of time to assure availability.

Clinton Wildlife Management Area and Spruce Run State Park surround most of the reservoir, offering thousands of acres of forest for hiking and biking. I found the most picturesque paddling to the south and southwest, where coves and peninsulas are most abundant and give you a better chance for solitude on crowded summer weekends. Hunterdon Sailing Club is based at the park and commonly holds regattas and other sailing events on weekends throughout

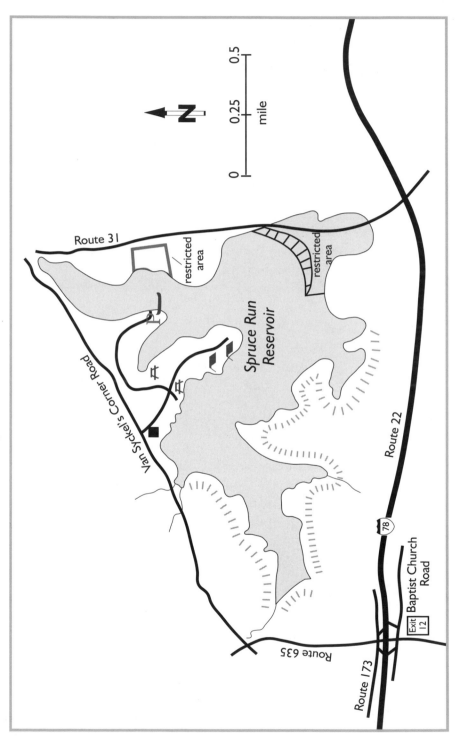

Spruce Run Reservoir

Route 31

restricted area

restricted area

Spruce Run Reservoir

Van Syckel's Corner Road

Route 22

Route 635

Route 173

Route 78

Exit 12

Baptist Church Road

N

0   0.25   0.5
         mile

Plan to camp here for a day or two to fully explore all the coves and peninsulas.

summer. Best bet for a secluded trip is to visit here off-season or on weekdays in summer.

Eagles, hawks, vultures, snakes, skunks, deer, foxes, and raccoons inhabit the forested lands. Along the tree-lined shores, you'll find numerous songbirds, bobolinks, blue jays, and warblers flitting about the branches overhanging the waters. Hybrid bass, pike, trout, and perch can be found in these waters, which extend down to 75 feet. I understand that hybrid bass give you a thrilling fight. While not an avid angler, I do take a fishing pole along a few times each year. Perhaps one day I'll hook a hybrid.

Lake Mercer
West Windsor (Mercer)

MAPS: New Jersey Atlas & Gazetteer, Map 42
  USGS Quadrangle, Princeton
AREA: 275 acres
INFORMATION: New Jersey Division of Fish and Wildlife, Central
  Region (Assunpink WMA), 386 Clarksburg–Robbinsville
  Road, Robbinsville, NJ 08691; 609-259-2132
HABITAT TYPE: open, with some woods
EXPECT TO SEE: waterfowl
TAKE NOTE: winds; electric motors only

GETTING THERE

From Route 571, drive south for 3.9 miles on Route 535. Turn right (west) onto Route 602 (South Post Road) into the park entrance and drive 1.1 miles to the marina entrance on the right. Take the first right to the launch site. The lower-level parking is for the big boats—the ones that need to be hauled by a trailer. After unloading your kayak or canoe, drive back up and around to the upper-level parking lot.

From Route 33, drive north 3.8 miles on Route 535. Turn left (west) onto Route 602 (South Post Road) and continue as above.

Mercer County Park is a huge complex located midway between Princeton and Trenton. The park's miles of rolling hills sprinkled with trees and woods have something for everyone, including golf, soccer, tennis, and, of course, boating. Set in the midst of the park is the 275-acre Lake Mercer with launch facilities, a small nature center, and restrooms. University sculling crews practice on the lake, and anglers come from miles around to try their luck. While most water activities occur in the central and western parts of the lake, the best paddling can be found on the eastern end, where thick woods line the shores. If you live around this highly populated area and want some large waters to paddle without traveling too far, this is the place.

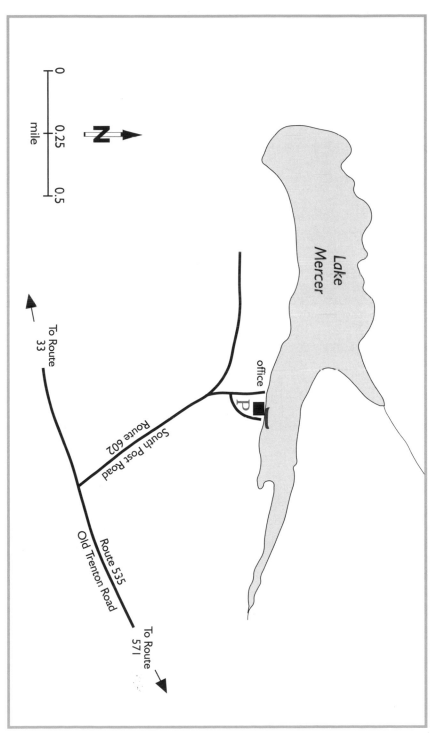

Lake Mercer

28

Lake Topanemus
Freehold (Monmouth)

MAPS: New Jersey Atlas & Gazetteer, Map 44
USGS Quadrangle, Freehold
AREA: 21 acres
INFORMATION: New Jersey Division of Fish and Wildlife, Central
Region (Assunpink WMA), 386 Clarksburg–Robbinsville
Road, Robbinsville, NJ 08691; 609-259-2132
HABITAT TYPE: woods
EXPECT TO SEE: turtles, waterfowl

GETTING THERE

From Route 522, drive north for 0.4 mile on Route 9, turn right (east), and drive 0.4 mile on Schibanoff Lane. Turn right (south) onto Waterworks Road and drive 0.1 mile. Turn left (east) onto Topanemus Lane, drive 0.2 mile, and turn left (north) onto Pond Road. Drive 0.5 mile to Lake Topanemus. The stone boat ramp is about 100 feet farther on the right, with an informal parking area on the left.

This quaint little lake is tucked away from the bustling activity of Route 9, just north of Freehold. Large oak and maple provide dense shade in the picnic and launch area, where a few lakeside benches invite you to sit and enjoy the scenery. A hiking trail leading from the east end of the parking area takes you through the woods and around most of the lake. Some private property is found across the lake from the launch, but the houses are set far back from the water. Launch your boat and head east (left) to enjoy an hour or more of lovely paddling along the wooded shores. Perhaps you'll pass painted or spotted turtles basking in the sun, or spot a kingfisher looking for dinner. The lake is stocked with largemouth bass, which swim among channel catfish, bluegill sunfish, and fathead minnows.

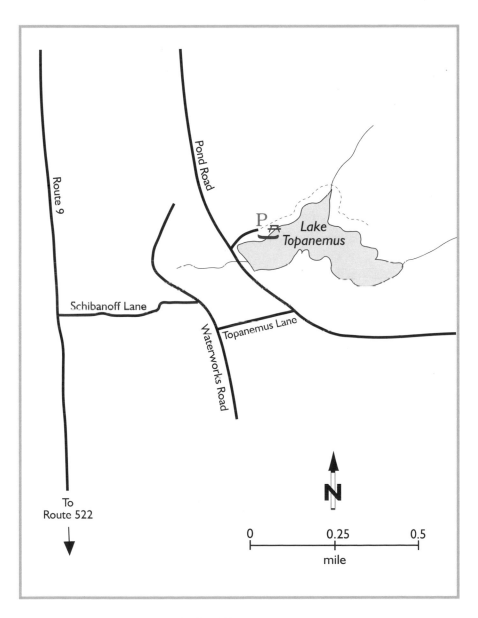

Lake Topanemus

29

Farrington Lake
New Brunswick (Middlesex)

MAPS: New Jersey Atlas & Gazetteer, Map 37
 USGS Quadrangle, New Brunswick
AREA: 290 acres
INFORMATION: New Jersey Division of Fish and Wildlife, Central
 Region (Assunpink WMA), 386 Clarksburg–Robbinsville
 Road, Robbinsville, NJ 08691; 609-259-2132
HABITAT TYPE: open, with some woods
EXPECT TO SEE: waterfowl, turtles, songbirds
TAKE NOTE: electric motors only

GETTING THERE

To the North Launch: From the New Jersey Turnpike, drive south for 0.4 mile on Route 130. Turn left onto Farrington Boulevard and drive for 0.4 mile to the parking area and launch.

 To the Central Launch: From the New Jersey Turnpike, drive south for 1.7 miles on Route 130, turn left onto Washington Avenue, and drive for 0.2 mile. A parking lot and launch site are right before the bridge.

Created by damming Lawrence Brook, this long, narrow lake is bordered on both sides by county parklands, where hiking trails meander through landscaped trees and shrubs. In the midst of a large metropolis, the park and its 290-acre lake provide a pleasant sanctuary from traffic, crowds, and industry for humans and wildlife. Goldfinches, cardinals, wrens, warblers, blue jays, and other songbirds seek refuge among the trees, while sunfish, perch, and catfish swim in the waters alongside stocked trout and bass. Electric outboards are permitted, but most fishing is done from shore. There are two good launch sites with ample parking and nearby picnic tables.

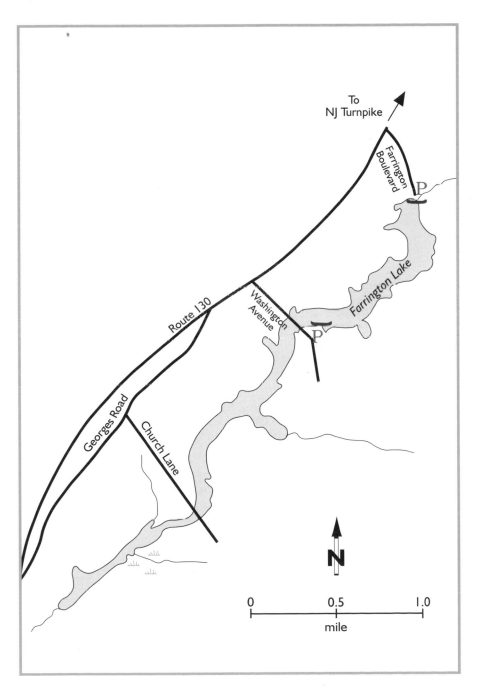

To
NJ Turnpike

Farrington Boulevard

P

Farrington Lake

Route 130

Washington Avenue

P

Georges Road

Church Lane

N

| 0 | 0.5 | 1.0 |

mile

Farrington Lake

Pitcher Plant

The carnivorous pitcher plant's common name is derived from the unusual shape of its leaf and its capacity to hold water. Sandy wetland soils are high in iron but low in nitrogen and other essential nutrients. Unusual plants such as pitchers and sundews have developed insect-eating adaptations to augment the inadequate supply of nitrogen in poor soil conditions. Hollow leaves retain water, while digestive juices first lure, then kill and slowly absorb unwary insects. Internal hairs point downward to hinder the insect's escape. The plant's diet consists of flies, moths, gnats, ants, bees, small butterflies, and even an occasional tiny frog. Leaves vary from yellow-green to deep purple, with dark red-purple veins.

While they can grow to 17 inches, most pitcher plants range between 6 and 12 inches. Leaves develop each year from stems that emerge from underground rhizomes and remain evergreen, making them easy to find during winter months. Reproduction is typically by seeds, with bees as the main pollinators, but may be accomplished by fragmentation of rhizomes.

Pitcher plants thrive in the acidic soils of savannas, flat woods near lakeshores, sphagnum moss and cedar bogs, and swamps—of which there are many in southern and central New Jersey. Spiders take advantage of the plant by spinning webs inside it to catch insects. Native Americans used the plant's root to treat tuberculosis and kidney ailments.

Another carnivorous plant to look for in moist and poor soils is the tiny sundew. It emits a sticky fluid that clings like dewdrops to catch and hold insects. Hairs press the victim down onto the surface of the blade, where it is then digested.

30

Turn Mill Lake, Lake Success, and Colliers Mill Lake

Colliers Mill (Ocean)

MAPS: New Jersey Atlas & Gazetteer, Map 49
USGS Quadrangle, Cassville
AREA: Turn Mill Lake, 100 acres
Lake Success, 40 acres
Colliers Mill Lake, 17 acres
INFORMATION: New Jersey Division of Fish and Wildlife, Central
Region (Assunpink WMA), 386 Clarksburg–Robbinsville
Road, Robbinsville, NJ 08691; 609-259-2132
HABITAT TYPE: woods, with some marsh areas
EXPECT TO SEE: hawks, eagles, waterfowl, deer, mountain laurel

---

GETTING THERE

From Route 70 near Whiting, drive 9.6 miles north on Route 539. Turn right onto Colliers Mill Road and drive 1.1 miles to the entrance of Colliers Mill Wildlife Management Area, which will be right in front of you. All roads are sandy and somewhat rutted. Parking is informal.

To Turn Mill Lake: From the entrance, drive 100 feet and turn right (south) onto the sand road. Drive 0.2 mile to the launch site on the left. Parking is available in a small clearing on the right, about 40 feet down the road.

To Colliers Mill Lake: From the entrance, drive straight ahead (east) for 0.2 mile and turn left. The launch and informal parking are right there.

To Lake Success: From Colliers Mill Lake, continue east on the main road for another 3.4 miles to the first launch area, which will be on the right. This is not the best launch site, because sugar-soft sand forces you to carry your boat about 75 feet, but the launch area is very pretty and makes a perfect informal picnic area under the shade of scrub pine trees. If you have four-wheel drive, you can drive about 50 feet closer for a shorter carry. The better launch site is another 0.2 mile around the lake, again on the right. Studded with pines, this also makes a nice informal picnic setting.

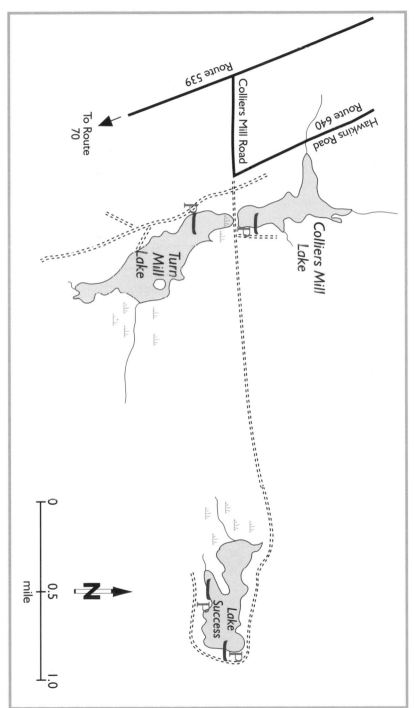

Turn Mill Lake, Lake Success, and Colliers Mill Lake

Remote and quiet, three lakes nestle into the landscape within Colliers Mill Wildlife Management Area. The surroundings are typical of the Pine Barrens pine and mixed oak-hardwood forests, with cedar, sweetgum, and red maple edging the water. Mountain laurel, sheep laurel, and the fragrant sweet pepperbush comprise most of the understory shrubs. The northern pine snake, whose range is primarily in and around South Carolina and Georgia, has small, disjunct colonies within the pinelands of New Jersey. Inhabiting only flat, sandy pine barrens, their secretive burrowing behavior eludes even the most experienced snake hunter. Pickerel, smallmouth bass, and sunfish live in the tea-colored waters typical of the Pine Barrens. Goldenrod flowers splash the landscape with yellow from late summer through fall, when they are joined by bouquets of wild blue asters.

Numerous coves edge Turn Mill Lake's 100 acres as you paddle to its southeastern end, where a few islands are tucked close to shore. The only drawback to the lake is that on some weekends local gun clubs use an established firing range for practice shooting. Though the range is not close, the sound echoes through the stillness. Should a gun club be present on the day you visit, you may want to drive out to Lake Success.

Turn Mill Lake is the largest of the three lakes at this site.

Cedar swamps on the northern end of Lake Success provide ample habitat for turtles, frogs, and songbirds.

Because it is highly washboarded, the road to Lake Success seems much longer than its 3.0 miles—I call it the "kidney test track." Pitch pine, cedar, and sweetgum border the lake's 40 acres, along with a number of beaches for informal picnics. Cedar swamps on its western end are ideal for bird watching. Numerous species of frogs, toads, and snakes relish this vast wilderness tract in the northern pinelands. Colliers Mill Lake lies just off the main sand road near the entrance and, although it's used as a picnic spot in summer, is never very crowded.

31

Whitesbog Ponds
Whitesbog (Ocean)

MAPS: New Jersey Atlas & Gazetteer, Map 49
   USGS Quadrangles, Browns Mill and Whiting
AREA: 53 acres
INFORMATION: New Jersey Division of Fish and Wildlife, Central
   Region (Assunpink WMA), 386 Clarksburg–Robbinsville
   Road, Robbinsville, NJ 08691; 609-259-2132
HABITAT TYPE: oak woods; open areas
EXPECT TO SEE: waterfowl, wading birds, songbirds, turtles
TAKE NOTE: cedar stumps abound in some areas

GETTING THERE

Getting there is easy; getting around inside the area can be challenging if you stray off the main road. All roads within the area are sand, and parts of them have deep ruts, so drive slowly. From Route 70, drive 1.1 miles northwest on Route 530, turn right onto Whitesbog Road, and drive 0.3 mile to the village.

The map here has been greatly simplified; the roads shown are those marked for the auto-tour trail through the complex. Follow them. A more detailed map is available at the information billboard in the center of Whitesbog Village.

If you love birding and butterflies, you'll love Whitesbog. Nature lovers from all over the state visit these exquisite bogs, which were once part of a privately owned cranberry operation. The area's history goes back to the mid–nineteenth century, when Colonel Fenwick purchased the land for experimental cranberry production. The farm soon became the largest cranberry producer in New Jersey, and in the late nineteenth century the family began blueberry farming on the drier land around the bogs. Colonel Fenwick's granddaughter, Elizabeth, worked on the farm with Dr. Frederick Colville to cultivate the blueberries. Many of today's blueberry strains in South Jersey originated

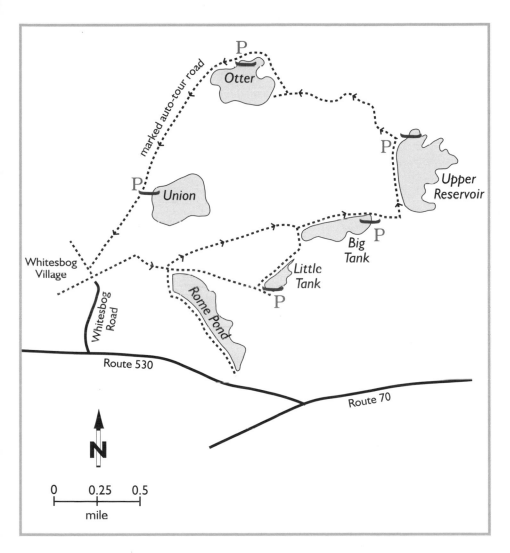

Whitesbog Ponds

from their venture. The state purchased the lands in the late 1960s with Green Acre funds and annexed the area to Lebanon State Forest. Projects funded by the New Jersey Division of Parks and Forestry and the Whitesbog Preservation Trust are restoring some of the original buildings in the tiny village.

Four attractive ponds and more than 10 miles of trails can take a few days to explore if you really stop to observe the wildlife. Birds and

White and yellow pond lilies carpet the launch site at Otter Pond.

butterflies thrive in and around the bogs, where rich supplies of berries, wildflowers, and fresh water provide them with an ideal habitat. Noted as a prime location to view the spring migration of neotropical song-birds, the area hosts year-round bird-watching walks sponsored by the New Jersey Audubon Society and various birding groups. Shallow pond waters and cedar stumps provide the perfect habitat for bog and painted turtles. Walking the open fields offers an opportunity to spot an eastern milk snake, whose black-bordered, reddish brown blotches stand out in striking contrast to its grayish tan body.

During summer, nodding heads of orange and red milkweed throw dashes of brilliant color on open grasslands, along with accents of deep blue loosestrife. In late summer, yellow goldenrod, blue aster, and soft purple joe-pye weed pick up the color accents. Whitesbog Village hosts a blueberry festival in July, where you can find blueberry pies, muffins, pancakes, and preserves.

～ 32 ～

Weequahic Lake
Newark (Union)

MAPS: New Jersey Atlas & Gazetteer, Map 32
USGS Quadrangle, Elizabeth

AREA: 80 acres

INFORMATION: New Jersey Division of Fish and Wildlife, Central
Region (Assunpink WMA), 386 Clarksburg–Robbinsville
Road, Robbinsville, NJ 08691; 609-259-2132

HABITAT TYPE: open, with some woods

EXPECT TO SEE: waterfowl

GETTING THERE

From East and North of the Park: Drive Route 22 west to the Frelinguysen/
Route 27 exit. Turn left at the end of the ramp onto Frelinguysen Avenue,
drive 0.2 mile, and turn right onto Noble Street. Drive one block to the T,
turn right onto Meeker Avenue, and drive for 200 feet to the park entrance
on the left.

From South and West of the Park: Take Route 22 east to the Hillside
Avenue/North Broad Street exit. Turn right at the end of the ramp and make
an immediate left onto North Broad Street. Stay in the right-hand lane.
North Broad Street becomes Elizabeth Street three blocks down, where you'll
see the park on the right. Continue straight on Elizabeth Street for 0.6 mile
(the end of the park) and turn right onto Meeker Avenue. The park entrance
is about 200 feet ahead on the right.

Weequahic Park is another gem in the midst of an urban area. An 80-
acre lake, its miles of hiking and biking trails, soccer fields, and picnic
areas transport you to a different world. The deeply scalloped south and
west sides offer the best paddling, with huge trees hugging the shores
beneath wooded hills. A local angler I talked with proudly displayed

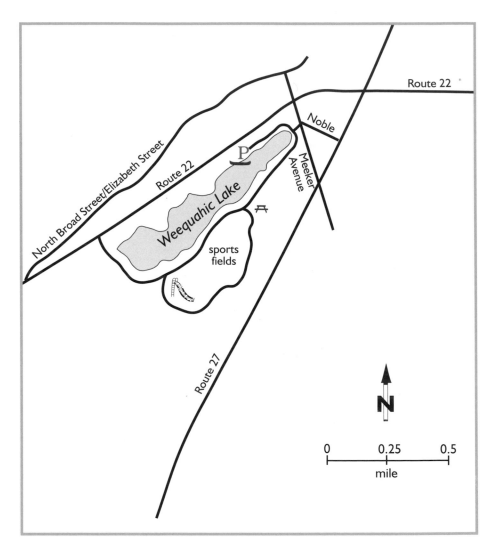

Weequahic Lake

the large carp he had caught earlier, saying, "There's lots o' big carp in these waters. Can catch one 'bout every day I come here." Sports fields and larger picnic areas are located far enough away so that only muffled sounds reach the lake.

Willow and beech trees border Weequahic Lake, noted for its huge carp.

Southern New Jersey

Pine Barrens: the term not only describes the environment but is also the formal name given to this vast area, which covers more than two-thirds of the land in the southern half of New Jersey. The Pine Barrens are recognized on every U.S. governmental level for its ecological importance and enormous water resources; in 1983 the United Nations officially designated close to one million acres—about one-quarter of New Jersey's total land area—the Pinelands National Reserve. The original Flemish settlers referred to this land as barren because traditional crops would not grow in the acidic conditions. These soils, however, provide a perfect environment for blueberry and cranberry growth, making New Jersey one of the leading producers for both fruits. Due to these barren lands and the numerous state forests and wildlife management areas acquired by the state over the past half century, southern New Jersey remains the least populated region in the state. To find out more about the Pine Barrens, contact Pinelands National Reserve, P.O. Box 7, 15 Springfield Road, New Lisbon, NJ 19106; 609-894-9342.

Enormous stands of Atlantic white cedar provided wood for a large shipbuilding industry in the mid-1900s. Shipbuilders Viking, Egg Harbor Yacht, and Ocean Yacht are still in existence today, though most of their boats are made of fiberglass. Behind the barrier islands rimming the Atlantic Ocean, vast expanses of tidal salt marshes create one of nature's most productive nursery grounds, offering nourishment and shelter for juvenile fish, crabs, and other inhabitants of coastal waters.

33

Batsto Lake
Pleasant Mills (Burlington)

MAPS: New Jersey Atlas & Gazetteer, Map 64
   USGS Quadrangle, Batsto
AREA: 40 acres
CAMPING: There is no camping around the lake, but there are several state-run campgrounds inside Wharton State Forest, plus a few private campgrounds in the vicinity. Stop in at the Batsto park office, located near Mile Marker 9 on Route 542, for camping information and a calendar of events. Camping is also available at Bel Haven Lake Resort Campground, 1213 Route 542, Green Bank, NJ 08215; 609-965-2827.
INFORMATION: Wharton State Forest, 4110 Nesco Road, Hammonton, NJ 08037; 609-561-0024
HABITAT TYPE: woods, bogs, and marshes
EXPECT TO SEE: waterfowl, wading birds, beaver, turtles, foxes, sweet pepperbush, wild iris

GETTING THERE

Access to the lake is from a sand road off Route 542 near Mile Marker 8 (but there is no Mile Marker 8 post) at the western end of Batsto Historical Village, where the split-rail fence surrounding the village turns back into the woods.

From Route 30: Drive east for 6.2 miles on Route 542 to where the road bends sharply to the right (east). At this bend you will see the wood split-rail fence that surrounds the historical village. Drive into the sandy clearing to the left of the fence and follow the sand road for 0.3 mile to the launch site. The road parallels the wood fence for about half of the drive. Parking space for about twelve vehicles is available next to the sandy ramp.

From Route 206: The turn-off to Batsto is exactly at Mile Marker 3. Turn left (you can't go right) onto Route 613 and proceed 2.4 miles to the first intersection. Turn left (a small brown Batsto sign is at the intersection), drive 0.3 mile to the T, and turn left onto Route 693. Hammonton airport will be immediately on the left (don't blink or you'll miss it). Continue straight (but

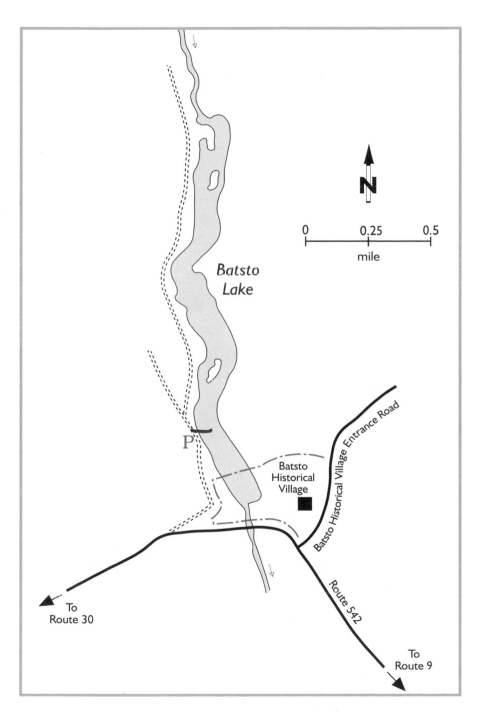

N

0   0.25   0.5
mile

Batsto Lake

Batsto Historical Village Entrance Road

Batsto
Historical
Village

P

To
Route 30

Route 542

To
Route 9

Batsto Lake

it's a crooked road) for 5.7 miles to the T; turn left onto Route 542 east and continue 3.9 miles to the sand entrance road.

From Northbound Garden State Parkway: Take Exit 50 onto north Route 9; Route 542 west intersects 1.3 miles up the road—be careful, this is a hairpin turn. Turn left onto Route 542 and drive 7.2 miles to the sand entrance road on the right. You will pass the Batsto Historical Village visitor center on the right about 0.6 mile before the boat access road.

From Southbound Garden State Parkway: Take Exit 52 and turn left at the end of the ramp onto East Greenbush. Drive for 3.0 miles to the T. Turn right (south) onto Route 9 and drive for 2.4 miles to its junction with Route 542 west (on the right). Near Mile Marker 9 on Route 542, the entrance road to the Batsto Historical Village visitor center will be on the right. Drive another 0.6 mile to the sand road on the right.

Nestled in Wharton State Forest in the heart of the Pine Barrens along Route 542, Batsto Historical Village offers a look at eighteenth- and nineteenth-century living when the village boomed with more than 200 residents. A dam was built in 1765 along the Batsto River, creating the present-day lake and bogs, to provide power to operate a blast furnace for the production of iron—the first commercial operation at Batsto. Bog iron "ore" begins to form when vegetative matter decays and settles in soils containing high amounts of soluble iron. The ensuing chemical reaction brings the iron in solution to the surface, where it oxidizes upon contact with air. The heavier oxidized iron then settles to the bottom as a reddish brown scum or sludge, cementing together bits of sand and gravel and then hardening to produce ironstone, or bog iron, in a process that takes about thirty years.

Surrounding forests provided the wood that was converted to charcoal to fuel the furnaces. Iron was used to make kitchenware items such as pots, stoves, and utensils, but the metal was in particular demand for the production of cannon and cannonballs during the French and Indian and Revolutionary Wars. In the mid–nineteenth century large deposits of coal in Pennsylvania proved more efficient to burn than charcoal. The discovery of better iron ore deposits in the west and the depletion of local bog iron beds forced the collapse of most ironwork furnaces in New Jersey.

Furnaces such as that in Batsto were then used in the production of glass, even though there were already a number of glass factories in

These two young friends have just completed their first kayaking experience. I'd say they're hooked.

existence in southern New Jersey. The sand in the state's southern region is composed primarily of silica, the basic ingredient in glass, and if there's one thing South Jersey has it's sand—and lots of it! Supposedly, the towns of Green Bank and Crowleytown produced a green glass from which the original mason jars were made. Both of these towns are located within 4.0 miles of Batsto Historical Village eastward along Route 542. A few remnants of old foundations on sandy back roads are all that remain of their furnace operations.

The launch site to Batsto Lake is on its southwestern end just outside the limits of Batsto Village. To the right of the launch will be a small dam and a few park buildings belonging to the village. You can paddle around there, but it is illegal to land on the property: signs are posted to this effect. To the left (north) it may look like the lake is very small and ends where the land juts out prominently, but paddle up the eastern edge and the larger portion of the lake will come into view. Two sandy beaches on the western shore of the northern end make great places to stop for lunch or just get out and stretch.

The first thing you may notice is the color of the water, a deep tea color typical of the Pine Barrens. Natural tannins and acids leached from cedar trees, coupled with the naturally high iron content of surrounding soils, stain the water this deep reddish brown. It may also leave a slight stain at the waterline on your boat, which is easily washed off. Lake depths generally average 3 to 6 feet, with slightly deeper waters where the river channel cuts through.

Around the lake you'll find a wide variety of dry upland and aquatic vegetation typical of the Pine Barrens. Oak and pine dominate the forest on the western and southern sides, along with a sprinkling of holly, tupelo, and sassafras. Red maple, swamp magnolia, sweetgum, and white cedar dominate in moist, low-lying areas. Swamp magnolias grace the landscape with large white blossoms that scent the air lightly from May through early July. The long, slender racemes of white flowers on sweet pepperbush release a refreshing fragrance detectable from 50 feet away. In fall crimson leaves of red maple join the vivid yellow, orange, and red-rust of sweetgums to provide a delightful contrast to the deep green cedar and pine. Mountain and sheep laurel, huckleberry, wild blueberry, sweet pepperbush, and chokeberry fill the understory. A great treat while paddling late June through early August is to scout the shoreline for blueberry bushes—and there are plenty of them. Wild blueberries are smaller than their cultivated counterparts, but much sweeter. Along the banks in late summer and fall, look for the matlike growth of wild cranberries, whose yellow-green berries start turning bright red in late September.

The northern section of the lake, particularly on the western side, becomes a shallow, swamplike environment. Here you want to paddle slowly or sit quietly, waiting for the birdlife to come to you. Cedar becomes more prominent, requiring moist or sodden soils. Fragrant white waterlilies and yellow pond lilies carpet the lake's surface in its coves, and its blue-purple spikes of flowers poke up from the arrow-shaped leaves of the pickerelweed.

Ospreys and turkey vultures frequent the northern half of the lake, along with grackles, fish crows, and various species of duck, the latter being more prominent in late summer and fall. If you're lucky, you'll get to see a bald eagle that has frequented the area for years. One of these days I'm going to find its nest. Great blue herons search the shallows for fish, while blue jays shriek through the trees. Warblers, swifts (I love them—they eat mosquitoes), gray catbirds, goldfinches, cardinals, rufous-sided towhees, woodpeckers, eastern phoebes, and eastern kingbirds are among the most frequently observed birds. Rufous-sided towhees are the most characteristic bird of upland pine barrens.

An abundant population of painted turtles, some of them quite large, sun themselves on fallen limbs and cedar stumps. Snapping turtles are common but rarely seen since they spend most of their time underwater. A number of beaver huts dot the length of the Batsto River. The southernmost one can be seen from the north end of the lake and usually features three or four large turtles hanging around on the firm sand near the water's edge.

Due to the high acidity and iron content of the water and its low nutrient level, fish and amphibian diversity is limited. Chain and redfin pickerel and yellow and brown bullheads (catfish) are about the only species fished for in this lake. The small blackbanded sunfish, with its striking black and white bands and angular body shape, is the most characteristic species of the Pine Barrens.

If you would like to get in a little hiking, the sandy road at the launch site continues north, paralleling the lake and river. Local livery services use it to drop paddlers off a few miles up the Batsto River. On a larger scale, the Batona Trail starts at Batsto Historical Village and travels northeast for 25 miles to Lebanon State Forest. You can hike all or part of this trail, which winds through dry upland pinelands, lowland swamps, and cranberry bogs. Be prepared for ticks while hiking, and check yourself frequently.

During summer, Batsto Historical Village hosts an antique car show, blueberry and cranberry festivals, and other family events, some of which include candle making, iron working, and other crafts of the bygone era. Pony rides and other activities for children are usually included.

34

Atsion Lake
Shamong (Burlington)

MAPS: New Jersey Atlas & Gazetteer, Map 56
   USGS Quadrangle, Atsion
AREA: 62 acres
CAMPING AND INFORMATION: Wharton State Forest/Atsion
   Office, 744 Route 206, Shamong, NJ 08088; 609-268-0444.
HABITAT TYPE: woods and swamp
EXPECT TO SEE: waterfowl, turtles, hawks, eagles

GETTING THERE

From Route 30, drive north for 7.3 miles on Route 206 and turn left into the recreation area. The boat ramp is on the far side of the parking lot. The park office is 0.3 mile north on the east (right) side of the road.

From Route 70, drive south for 10.2 miles on Route 206, turn right into the entrance, and proceed as above.

One of the larger lakes within the 110,000-acre Wharton State Forest, Atsion Lake (pronounced AT-*zon* by locals) is the only one that provides on-site camping facilities, many of which are lakeside. White waterlilies carpet the shallower western end, where the headwaters of the Mullica River, the largest waterway in the Pine Barrens, feed into the lake.

Thick pine and oak woods surround the lake, with a few stands of *Phragmites* along shallower shores. Red maple, hickory, and birch trees poke their branches between dark green pine and cedar at the water's edge, creating a colorful contrast in fall. Most of the lake is fairly deep by coastal plain standards, with some spots reaching depths of 15 feet or more.

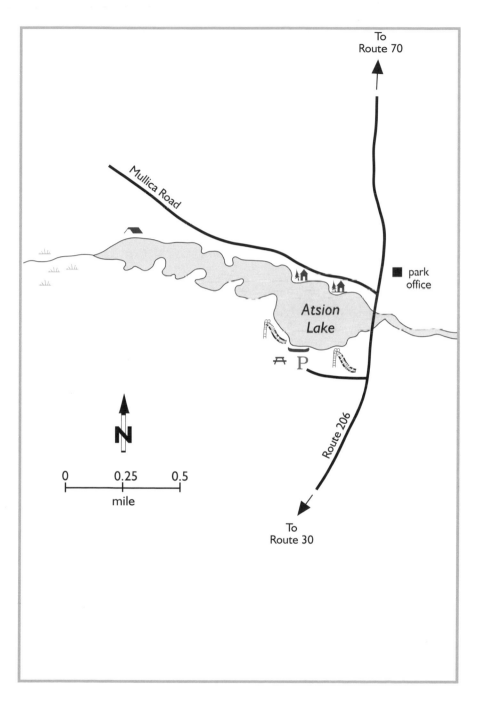

To
Route 70

Mullica Road

park
office

Atsion
Lake

P

N

0   0.25   0.5
mile

Route 206

To
Route 30

Atsion Lake

Cedar and sweet gum line the shores of Atsion Lake.

Nine lakeside log cabins, each offering a private car-top launch, are available on the northeastern end of the lake, and a large campground on the northwestern end offers a few on-water sites. A public boat launch, playgrounds, showers, swimming beach, nature trails, and picnic facilities are provided at the recreation area on the south side of the lake.

Pine Barrens Tree Frog

Occurring nowhere else in New Jersey, the chorus of the Pine Barrens tree frogs fills the air on late-spring evenings during breeding season. They inhabit shallow pools in sphagnum bogs, backwater and slow-moving streams, cranberry bogs, and cedar swamps. Requiring acidic environments, the tree frog's habitat is susceptible to any human infringement that raises water pH levels or decreases the water table. Considered a threatened species, preservation of the tree frog's specific wetland habitat is crucial for survival. Only a few other disjunct populations have been found in the acidic bogs of the Carolinas, Georgia, and western Florida.

Lavender stripes bordered in white create a striking contrast to the tree frog's emerald-green 1.5-inch-long body. Bright yellow and orange conceal the surfaces of its legs. As is indicative of tree frogs, its long, webbed toes end in adhesive discs that enable it to cling to twigs and bark. Insects and other invertebrates found in moist environments constitute its main diet. Males produce a nasally *quonk-quonk-quonk* sound through vocal sacs that inflate like a balloon. Though heard in vast numbers, the tree frog is difficult to find unless you patiently follow the call to its source. Breeding and egg laying take place in May and June, with the larvae metamorphosing into adults by July to early August. Due to their secretive lives, little is known about tree frog behavior outside the breeding season.

～35～
Mannington Meadows
Pennsville (Salem)

MAPS: New Jersey Atlas & Gazetteer, Maps 60 and 61
   USGS Quadrangles, Salem and Penns Grove
AREA: 2,000-plus acres
INFORMATION: Supawna Meadows National Wildlife Refuge, 229
   Lighthouse Road, Salem, NJ 08079; 609-935-1487
HABITAT TYPE: brackish marsh
EXPECT TO SEE: waterfowl, shorebirds, wading birds, eagles,
   ospreys, pickerelweed
TAKE NOTE: motorboats

GETTING THERE

From Route 49 on the southeast end of Pennsville, drive north on Route 551 (Hook Road) for 2.0 miles. Turn right onto East Pittsfield Street and drive 0.7 mile to the boat launch and parking at the end of the road.

From the north, take I-295 or the New Jersey Turnpike south. The two highways come together for a short span right before the Delaware Memorial Bridge. Follow signs for the Pennsville/Salem/Last Exit Before Toll ramp. Drive 0.3 mile and turn left, following signs that read, Hook Road/40 East to Tpk. and Atlantic City Expy. Drive 0.5 mile, following the signs to Hook Road. The road will bend to the right and put you onto Hook Road. Drive for 1.2 miles, turn left onto East Pittsfield, and continue for 0.8 mile to the launch—the blacktop will end about halfway to the end. Parking is informal.

Neither a lake nor a bay, Mannington Meadows' vast expanse of brackish waters can fill days of paddling enjoyment for the nature lover. Situated close to the Delaware River, these waters are slightly tidal.

A tortuous network of narrow channels at the mouth of the Salem River snakes its way around tiny islands and buffers most of the tidal current effect. You'll notice as the day wears on a slightly higher or lower waterline along the shores. With more than 3,000 acres in this

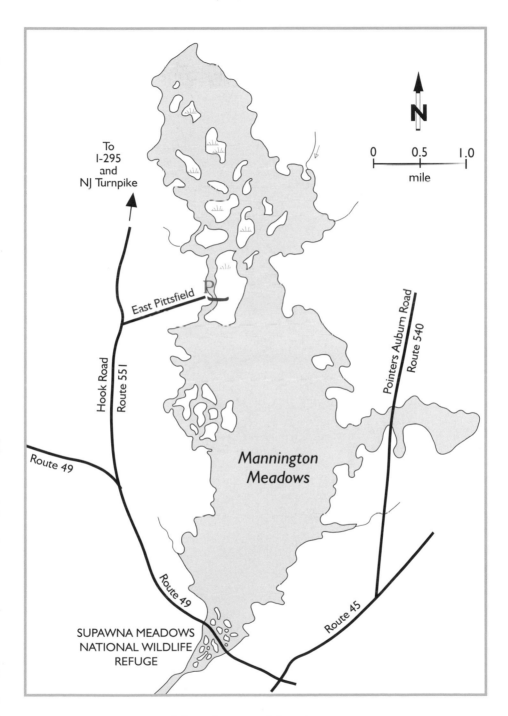

To
I-295
and
NJ Turnpike

East Pittsfield

P

Hook Road

Route 551

Pointers Auburn Road

Route 540

N

0   0.5   1.0
mile

Route 49

*Mannington
Meadows*

Route 49

Route 45

SUPAWNA MEADOWS
NATIONAL WILDLIFE
REFUGE

Mannington Meadows

Looking through one of the many coves in the brackish marshes on Mannington Meadows.

low-lying coastal plain, you will probably need to push yourself off a sandbar or two when the tide is out, particularly in the narrower side channels. Deeper waters lie along the eastern shoreline, where the Salem River has cut a deep channel. Supawna Meadows National Wildlife Refuge adjoins Mannington Meadows along the latter's south-western flank. The refuge provides wintering and migrating waterfowl with an important feeding and resting area.

Egrets, herons, shorebirds, pintails, black ducks, cormorants, woodcocks, songbirds, and a plethora of other bird species are common visitors. Ospreys and wood ducks that nest at the nearby refuge come to Mannington Meadows often to hunt. Frogs, turtles, and muskrats are abundant along the shallower eastern shores, where they live among wide fields of waterlilies and marsh grasses. Look for the diamondback terrapin, one of the few turtles that inhabit brackish waters on a consistent basis.

The launch is located along a channel in the northwestern end of the meadows. Paddle right to enter the meadows proper, or paddle left into channels, where you're likely to see muskrats—or at least evidence that they live here.

36

Stafford Forge Ponds
Stafford Forge (Ocean)

MAPS: New Jersey Atlas & Gazetteer, Map 65
USGS Quadrangle, West Creek

AREA: Pond 1, 48 acres
Pond 2, 22 acres
Pond 3, 73 acres

CAMPING: Sea Pirate Campground is located on the east side of
Route 9, 5.0 miles south of Route 72. Sea Pirate Campground,
P.O. Box 271, West Creek, NJ 08092; 609-296-7400.

INFORMATION: New Jersey Division of Fish and Wildlife,
Southern Region (Winslow WMA), 229 Blue Anchor Road,
Sicklerville, NJ 08081; 856-629-0090

HABITAT TYPE: open woods, cedar bogs, and marshes

EXPECT TO SEE: ospreys, waterfowl, wading birds

TAKE NOTE: electric motorboats only

GETTING THERE

From Route 72, drive south for 3.7 miles on Route 9 and turn right onto
Forge Road (there will be a sign for Stafford Forge Wildlife Management
Area). Drive 1.9 miles and turn right onto the sand entrance road. *Caution:*
Watch for what locals call "sugar sand"—a very soft sand known to swallow
even tow trucks whole. Only a few small spots of it are found on the main
roads, but they are prevalent on other back roads should you go exploring.

To Pond 1: From the entrance, make an immediate left and drive 0.3 mile
to the end. Put in anywhere on the sandy tip. Parking is informal.

To Ponds 2 and 3: From the entrance, stay to the right and follow the
road around for 0.6 mile, turn left, and drive 0.4 mile to the other end of the
sand dike. As you pass over the dike, pond #3 will be on the right, pond #2
on the left. A hard-sand launch for pond #3, the largest and deepest of the
ponds, will be on the right at the end of the dike. Parking is informal. Pond
#2 is accessed by turning left at the end of the dike—drive 0.2 mile and launch
from the sandy ramp.

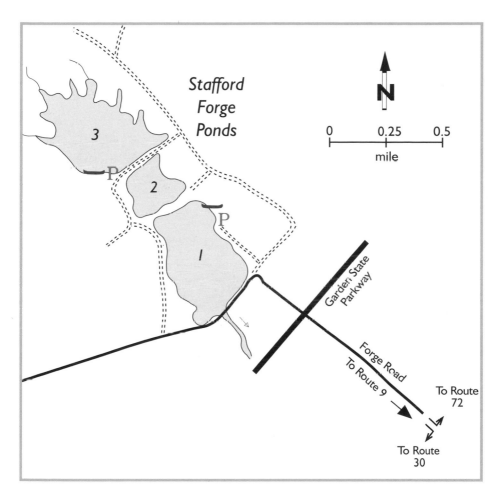

Stafford Forge Ponds

Stafford Forge Wildlife Management Area is home to three ponds, originally cranberry bogs, where countless herons, egrets, ducks, and other water birds inhabit the rich environment. Atlantic white cedar, sweetgum, and red maple dominate the scenery near the water, along with an occasional plush stand of *Phragmites* and cattails. Typical Pine Barren forests of mixed oaks and pitch pine fill the surrounding woods for miles. If you want solitude, this is it. Electric outboards are permitted, though I've never seen one, and hunting is allowed during specific seasons.

Pitch pine and oak stand behind cedar in the northernmost pond.

Listen for the telltale *eep, eep* of the ospreys that frequently fish these waters, especially in Pond 1. If you do spot an osprey, keep an eye on it for a while—seeing one plunge into the water and come out with a fish in its talons is a rewarding experience. Great blue herons, great egrets, and mallards are the more common water birds here, while blue jays, warblers, and grackles regularly inhabit the woods. Small coves created by inlet streams dot the southern and northern shores of Pond 3, the largest and deepest of the Stafford Forge ponds.

Late summer and early fall are the prettiest months to visit. Fluffy *Phragmites* heads laden with seeds shimmer silvery-beige against a background of dark green cedar. Here and there swamp-loving cardinal flowers add stokes of vibrant red, and water grasses turn a deep gold to rust. Mulberry bushes become deep scarlet, and sweetgum trees splash vibrant yellow, orange, and red around the ponds. Be aware that in an extreme drought year, the normally shallow 3- to 5-foot-deep waters can become nothing more than giant puddles.

37

Newton Lake and Cooper River Park Lake
Collingswood (Camden)

MAPS: New Jersey Atlas & Gazetteer, Map 54
   USGS Quadrangle, Camden
AREA: Cooper River Park Lake, 150 acres
   Newton Lake, 40 acres
INFORMATION: New Jersey Division of Fish and Wildlife,
   Southern Region (Winslow WMA), 229 Blue Anchor Road,
   Sicklerville NJ 08081; 856-629-0090
HABITAT TYPE: Cooper River Park Lake, woods and a
   corporate park
   Newton Lake, open woods with some development
EXPECT TO SEE: wading birds, turtles
TAKE NOTE: electric motorboats only on both lakes

GETTING THERE

To Cooper River Park Lake: From the Routes 130/30 circle, drive north for 0.4 mile on Route 130, turn right onto South Park Drive, and continue for 0.9 mile to the boat launch and parking area on the left. An additional car-top launch can be found 1.0 mile down South Park Drive just after crossing Cuthbert Boulevard. Park your car and carry your boat about 20 feet to the grassy bank.

To launch from the north shore at the pagoda, drive north for 0.6 mile on Route 130 from the Routes 130/30 circle. Turn right onto North Park Drive and drive for 2.3 miles, crossing Cuthbert Boulevard along the way.

To Newton Lake: From the Routes 130/30 circle, drive east for 0.7 mile on Route 30, turn left onto Newton Park Drive (it's Newton Avenue on the right), and drive 0.45 mile to Coleford Street. A small stone dock is on the lake directly across from Coleford Street. Leave your vehicle on Newton Park Drive on the lake side as close as possible to Coleford Street. Parking is curbside, parallel to the road by the lake. If you can park at the launch site, you'll only have a 40-foot portage, but expect a longer carry if you visit on a crowded day and need to park farther away.

Newton Lake and Cooper River Park Lake

A great egret walks along the shallow edges of Newton Lake between rafts of pickerelweed.

Newton Lake is another attractive lake in the midst of a highly populated area. The rim of a municipal park of the same name surrounds the 40-acre lake. Walking paths weave their way around trees along the landscaped swath of land dotted with lakeside benches and small gardens. Long and narrow, the lake's serpentine shape provides a long, relaxing paddle.

Over the years the city has cleaned up the Cooper River's waters and created a lovely park along a 2.5-mile stretch where it widens to a few hundred yards—enough to call it a lake at least by South Jersey standards. For those who live in the densely populated Camden area and need a place to paddle close to home, this section of the river landscaped with trees, shrubs, and small garden areas provides the perfect refuge. The best paddling is on the eastern end, where the shores become more wooded and you're farther from bustling traffic. Biking and hiking trails snake their way along both shores, and portable toilets are conveniently located all along the grounds.

One launch spot on the east end of the north shore has a small pagoda set slightly back from the water's edge, creating an attractive setting. The park is closed from midnight until 6 A.M., leaving plenty of time for a moonlight paddle. A large concrete boat ramp with ample parking is available on the south shore.

38

Shaw's Mill Pond
Newport (Cumberland)

Maps: New Jersey Atlas & Gazetteer, Map 68
USGS Quadrangle, Cedarville
Area: 30 acres
Information: New Jersey Division of Fish and Wildlife,
Southern Region (Winslow WMA), 229 Blue Anchor Road,
Sicklerville, NJ 08081; 856-629-0090
Habitat Type: woods and open areas, with some development
Expect to See: waterfowl, wading birds, turtles
Take Note: electric motorboats only

Getting There

From Route 610, drive south for 2.7 miles on Route 553 (Main Street), turn left onto Baptist Road, and drive for 0.5 mile. Bear left at the fork—this is Newport Station Road, but there is no sign—and drive 0.4 mile to the pond. The road turns left here, but you want to drive to the right onto the sand parking area and launch, both of which are informal. To reach another access, get back on the road and drive another 0.1 mile, passing over the creek bridge. Turn right after the bridge onto the sand area.

Fortesque, a town on the Delaware Bay known throughout most of South Jersey for its fantastic crabbing industry, lies only a short distance from Shaw's Mill Pond. It's worth a trip to the little village after paddling the pond, where you will enjoy exploring the numerous inlets and coves in this isolated setting surrounded by woods. Bass, pickerel, and perch swim beneath the quiet waters. Miles of hiking trails on the east side of the pond wind through woods set aside to protect wildlife habitat; no vehicles are permitted on roads through the area. Gas motors are prohibited on the pond.

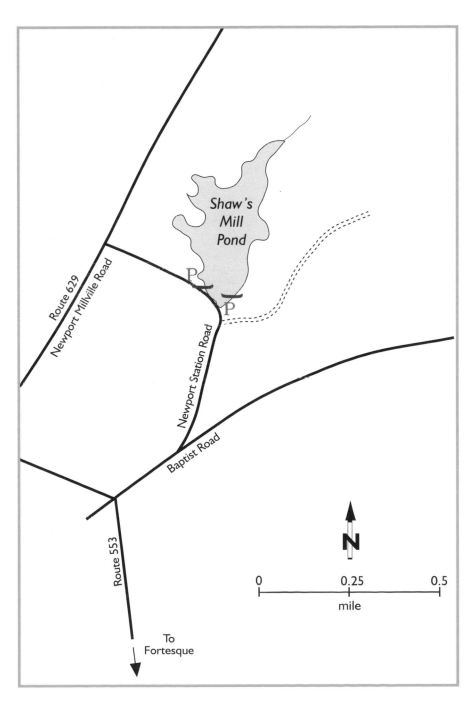

Shaw's Mill Pond

39

Manahawkin Impoundment and Bridge to Nowhere
Manahawkin (Ocean)

MAPS: New Jersey Atlas & Gazetteer, Map 59
USGS Quadrangle, Ship Bottom

AREA/LENGTH: Manahawkin Impoundment, 35 acres
Bridge to Nowhere, 10-plus miles of meandering channels

INFORMATION: New Jersey Division of Fish and Wildlife,
Southern Region (Winslow WMA), 229 Blue Anchor Road,
Sicklerville, NJ 08081; 856-629-0090

HABITAT TYPE: coastal marsh and lowland woods

EXPECT TO SEE: shorebirds, wading birds, waterfowl, ospreys,
turtles, foxes

TAKE NOTE: Manahawkin Impoundment—electric motorboats
only; Bridge to Nowhere—motorboats, wind, tides

GETTING THERE

To Manahawkin Impoundment: From Route 72, drive north for 0.1 mile on Route 9 to the Bay Avenue traffic light. One hundred feet north of Bay Avenue, turn right onto Stafford Road and drive 0.8 miles to Hillard Boulevard. From there, Stafford Road continues straight as a rough washboard sand road—go slow. Continue for another 1.5 miles; the small launch to the impoundment will be on the right. The road widens slightly here for parking, which is casual. Park parallel to the road and close to roadside vegetation so other cars can pass easily.

To Bridge to Nowhere: Continue down Stafford Road for another 0.6 mile to the end. A wooden bridge spans the creek. Launch from the left side of the bridge, where you'll see a narrow path leading to the creek.

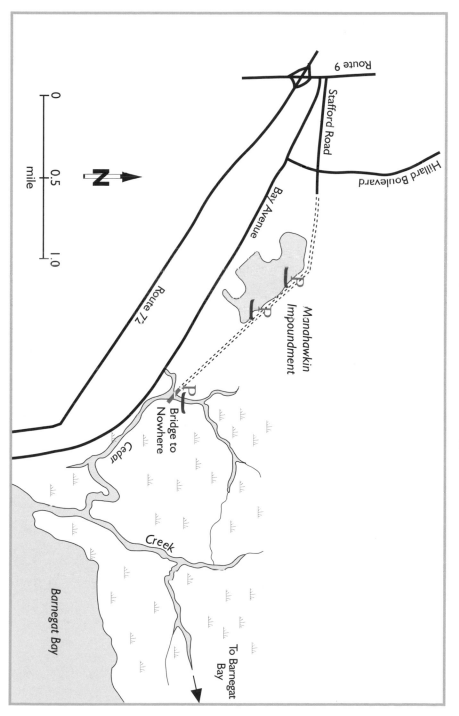

Manahawkin Impoundment and Bridge to Nowhere

Route 9

Stafford Road

Hillard Boulevard

Bay Avenue

Route 72

Manahawkin
Impoundment

P

P

P

Bridge to
Nowhere

Cedar

Creek

Barnegat Bay

To Barnegat
Bay

N

0   0.5   1.0
mile

So where does the Bridge to Nowhere go? Just where its name implies; hence the funky moniker locals gave this part of Barnegat National Wildlife Refuge. Situated far from inlets, so that tidal currents have minimal effect, this is an excellent spot to explore the salt marshes and backwaters of Barnegat Bay. From the launch next to the bridge, paddle to the right (south) down the meandering channel leading to the bay. Once you exit the channels it would be wise to turn around, get your bearings, and note landmark positions before paddling in the open waters. Since the marsh area sticks out prominently, it's easy to find your way back, but you'll have more peace of mind if you take that extra step on your first few trips here. You also can turn left from the launch into a maze of channels if you feel adventurous and have a good sense of direction.

Snowy and great egrets are abundant in the shallow waters along the banks, along with an occasional great blue heron. Narrow side channels lead into the wider main channel along the way; check them out when you pass, because sandpipers and egrets often prefer these more secluded waters.

Egrets, herons, and swans are frequent visitors to the impoundment.

Tidal saltwater marshes on the mainland side of Barnegat Bay provide a refuge for wading and shorebirds.

Tall reeds and a smattering of bayberry bushes rim the shores around Manahawkin Impoundment. Marsh wrens, tough birds to spot, fill the air with their nervous, high-pitched twitter from inside dense *Phragmites* stands. Between the reeds and the oak-dominated lowland woods behind them, cedar and red maple take hold on the moist middle ground. The impoundment is small, but it makes a delightful side trip on the way to the Bridge to Nowhere. Swans and ducks swim on the waters, and cedar waxwings usually can be spotted on the dense clusters of cedar on the far end.

Snowy Egret

At first glance the snowy egret might be confused with the great egret, another member of the family *Ardeidae* with stark white feathers, black legs, and a long, slender neck. But the great egret, in addition to being much larger, sports a yellow beak and black toes; the snowy egret has a black beak and yellow toes. Avid birders refer to snowy egrets as "snegs" and great egrets as "gregs." Members of *Ardeidae* have several things in common: long necks that fold into an S-shape in flight, spearlike bills, and legs that trail when flying. Adult snowy egrets have shaggy heads, necks, and back plumes that are clearly visible when not in flight—almost as if they forgot to comb their hair.

Snowy egrets typically frequent wetland environments such as salt marshes, and brackish marshes, ponds, and swamps within the coastal plain. While it is not unusual to spot a solitary egret, they are more often found in small colonies, foraging for food. Occasionally they maintain their own separate feeding territory. If you hear a lot of low croaking and see some feathers rustling, chances are that a snowy egret feels its territory has been infringed upon.

Commensal feeding, in which one species gives a feeding advantage to another, is prevalent among snowy egrets and ibises and other herons. Most egrets and herons forage in a "stalk and strike" method. While they may initially stalk, snowy egrets shuffle their feet in a flurry to stir up aquatic invertebrates, a favorite prey. In the process, many creatures are sent scurrying and made available to other birds foraging within a few feet. Small fish, reptiles, and insects are also hunted in lesser quantities.

The long ornamental head that snowy egrets develop during breeding season almost caused their demise in the late nineteenth and early twentieth centuries, when large colonies of snowy, red, and great egrets were killed for these special feathers, which were used to make ladies' hats. The plumes also were highly sought after as ornaments in Asian ceremonial dress. In 1901 the National Audubon Society sponsored a law prohibiting the killing of any bird except game birds. In the Everglades, where large breeding colonies existed, a labyrinth of narrow channels filled with mosquitoes and alligators proved impossible to patrol. As a result, plume hunters continued to make money as species counts dwindled. In 1903 plumes sold for $32 an ounce—more than the price of gold at the time!

Soon, however, public outcry inspired additional protections, and the bird was able to make a marked comeback.

East Creek Pond and Lake Nummy
Woodbine (Cape May)

MAPS: New Jersey Atlas & Gazetteer, Map 72
    USGS Quadrangles, East Creek Pond, Heislerville, Lake
    Nummy, and Woodbine
AREA: East Creek Pond, 62 acres
    Lake Nummy, 26 acres
CAMPING: Belleplain State Forest, County Route 550, P.O. Box
    450, Woodbine, NJ 08270; 609-861-2404
HABITAT TYPE: oak and pine lowland woods; cedar bogs
EXPECT TO SEE: waterfowl, ospreys, egrets and herons, turtles
TAKE NOTE: electric motors only on both ponds

GETTING THERE

To Lake Nummy and the Visitor Center: From Route 47 on the south side of Woodbine, drive north for 3.1 miles on Route 557, turn left (west) onto Route 550, and drive 1.4 miles to the park entrance on the left. The visitor center will be on the right about 100 feet inside the park. Continue past the visitor center for 0.35 mile, turn right onto Meisle Road, and drive 0.4 mile to the dock at Lake Nummy. You may park next to the boat ramp.

To East Creek Pond: From Route 557, drive north for 0.7 mile on Route 47. The road forks here, with Route 47 going to the left and Route 347 to the right. Take the right fork onto Route 347 and drive for 2.0 miles. Turn right into the boat ramp area on the right at the end of the guardrail. You may park here.

Miles and miles of hiking trails meander through more than 15,000 acres of upland oak and pine forests, hardwood forests, Atlantic white cedar swamps, and bogs within Belleplain State Forest. Situated on the outskirts of Pine Barren lands, the better soil conditions here allow for a wider variety of trees and shrubs, including hickory, beech, and ash. Two bodies of water, East Creek Pond and Lake Nummy, lie completely

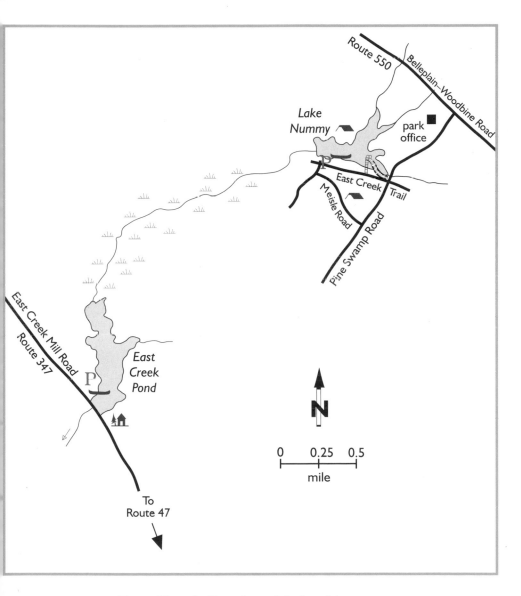

East Creek Pond and Lake Nummy

within the park's boundaries. The smaller of the two, Lake Nummy, centers on the park's campground, swimming beach, and recreational area on the east and south shores and becomes quite crowded in summer. Part of the north end of the lake ducks under a footpath bridge, making a quaint little paddle for novices or parents taking their children out for the first time.

Two friends enjoy a lazy afternoon of paddling along the coves in East Creek Pond.

A group cabin sits off a small county road near the short southern end of East Creek Pond. Numerous coves and inlets house large populations of painted and bog turtles, which bask in the sun on logs and cedar stumps. In summer sweet pepperbush develops racemes of white flowers, which fill the air with a sweet aroma detectable for more than 50 feet. For a sweet snack in July and August, look for blueberry bushes that peek out along the edge of the lake. Arrow weed, pickerelweed, and waterlilies along the shallower shores provide a protective environment for the young pickerel, smallmouth bass, sunfish, and crappies found in the lake.

Tent and trailer campsites are available, but only the group cabin at East Creek Pond is on the water. Yurts, a type of circular tent with wood floors, a deck, and a Plexiglas skylight, are also available for rent. No gas motors are permitted on the lakes.

~ 41 ~

Great Bay and the Edwin B. Forsythe National Wildlife Refuge
Smithville (Atlantic)

Maps: New Jersey Atlas & Gazetteer, Map 65
USGS Quadrangle, Oceanville
Length: 15-plus miles of meandering channels
Camping: Evergreen Woods Lakefront Resort, P.O. Box 250, 106 East Moss Mill Road, Pomona, NJ, 08240; 609-652-1577. From Scott's Landing, return to Route 9 and continue west on Alternate Route 561 for 3.2 miles. The campground will be on the left.
Information: Edwin B. Forsythe National Wildlife Refuge, Box 72, Oceanville, NJ 08231; 609-652-1665
Habitat Type: brackish marsh
Expect to See: ospreys, shorebirds, wading birds, hawks, songbirds, terrapins
Take Note: motorboats; tides

GETTING THERE

The Scott's Landing boat ramp is located east of Smithville on Route 9.

From the South: From Route 30, drive north for 3.2 miles on Route 9, turn right (east) onto Alternate Route 561 (Moss Mill Road), and drive 1.5 miles. The road turns to the left here. Drive around the bend and take the next right, about 100 feet away. Follow this road for 0.4 mile. The parking area will be on the left; the concrete boat ramp will be about 100 feet straight ahead.

From the North: Take Garden State Parkway Exit 48, which puts you onto Route 9 south. Drive for 6.7 miles and turn left onto Route 561. Continue as above.

This is one of those coastal bay areas I could not help but include because of its prodigious numbers of bird species, which can be observed year-round. Edwin B. Forsythe National Wildlife Refuge is

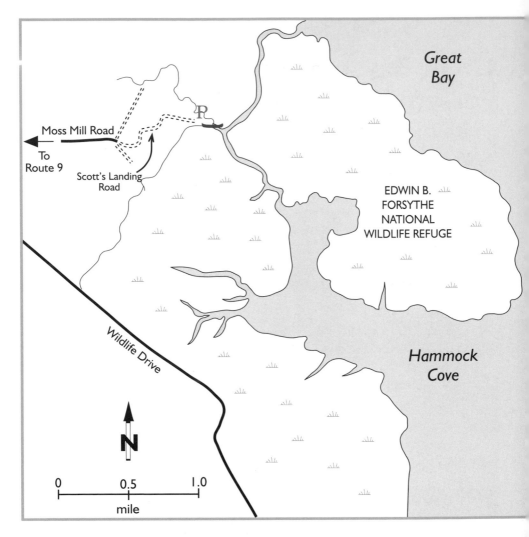

Great Bay and the Edwin B. Forsythe National Wildlife Refuge

one of the major stopovers along the Atlantic flyway for migratory birds. You will paddle out through the salt marshes and on into the back side of Great Bay. Spring and fall migrations bring large numbers of shorebirds, waterfowl, and wading birds to rest and feed before continuing their journey. Some remain for the entire summer. Diamondback terrapins, with their decorative concentric whorls, are found frequently in and around the marshes. Look skyward for bald eagles, ospreys, peregrine falcons, and hawks.

From mid-May to early June, migrating birds feast on horseshoe crab eggs in the Chesapeake and Delaware Bay estuaries; this refuge provides their next major stopover. One of my favorite early-summer migratory species is the Arctic tern—travelers from South America that stop here for a few weeks prior to continuing their journey to the Arctic. That's a total distance of 10,000 miles or more! In mid-October the sky is filled with flocks of snow geese—large white birds with black-tipped wings. In winter black ducks, Atlantic brants, and Canada geese dominate the ponds.

On the nearby barrier islands, beaches and dunes provide nesting habitat for piping plovers, black skimmers, and least terns. Watch for posted signs if you decide to explore these islands; a few are primary nesting sites for the piping plover and off-limits during nesting season.

For the quickest trip to the refuge, paddle south (right) from the launch area. It's only about a 3.0-mile paddle to Hammock Cove on the north side of the refuge. You will probably see a car or two driving down the north dike.

For a longer, more scenic trip, paddle north (left) from the launch area for about 1.0 mile to the bay. Once you're about 200 feet out into

A family of kayakers paddle slowly near a flock of egrets.

Cormorants swim underwater to catch their prey. Unlike ducks, their feathers are not waterproof, so they must "dry out" occasionally.

the bay, stop to notice the entrance to the creek you just exited and any visuals, such as channel markers and lights buoys. Never rely on inland coastal charts—a good storm can destroy or move markers. Take note of where markers are today. Paddle south (right) around the salt marsh peninsula and into Hammock Cove, a distance of about 6.0 miles.

The drive-through part of the refuge can be reached by traveling south for about 7.6 miles on Route 9 from Smithville to Oceanville. A large refuge sign on Route 9 directs you to the entrance. Open from dawn until dusk, the 8.0-mile vehicle loop takes you past upland fields and woodlands, coastal salt meadows and marshes, open bays, and channels. Two observation towers are located along the drive, the second of which is closer to the large human-made peregrine nesting house. The visitor center, open 8 A.M. to 4 P.M. weekdays and weekends, displays numerous wildlife exhibits. Two short nature trails are located adjacent to the center—bring lots of mosquito repellent July through September. A small entrance fee is charged to enter the drive loop.

～42～

Union Lake
Millville (Cumberland)

MAPS: New Jersey Atlas & Gazetteer, Map 68
   USGS Quadrangle, Millville
AREA: 898 acres
INFORMATION: New Jersey Division of Fish and Wildlife,
   Southern Region (Winslow WMA), 229 Blue Anchor Road,
   Sicklerville, NJ 08081; 856-629-0090
HABITAT TYPE: lowland woods, with some shoreline
   development
EXPECT TO SEE: waterfowl, hawks, deer, raccoons
TAKE NOTE: winds; motorboats limited to 10 HP

GETTING THERE

From Route 55 near Millville, take Exit 29 (Sherman Avenue) and turn west
onto Sherman Avenue. Drive 2.5 miles, turn left onto Route 608 (Carmel
Avenue), and drive for 3.4 miles to the Union Lake Wildlife Management
Area on the left. Continue for 0.2 mile to the parking area and concrete ramp.
Portable toilets are available Memorial Day through Labor Day. For a wood-
sier launch, drive to the far end of the parking lot, where a wide trail leads to
a small, sandy area about 50 feet from the parking lot.

   If you come by way of Route 49 (Main Street), Carmel Avenue veers off
Route 49 about 1.8 miles west of Route 47. Drive 1.2 miles on Carmel
Avenue to the lake entrance on the right.

Located in the southeast corner of Cumberland County on the western
outskirts of Millville, Union Lake was created by the damming of the
Maurice and Mill Rivers. This oblong lake covers 898 acres and is 4.0
miles long and 1.2 miles at its widest point. The state acquired the lake
in the early 1990s; it is now a fish and wildlife management area. As at
many other waterways in the state, Native American artifacts have been
found here. The Vineland Historical and Antiquarian Society, at Seventh

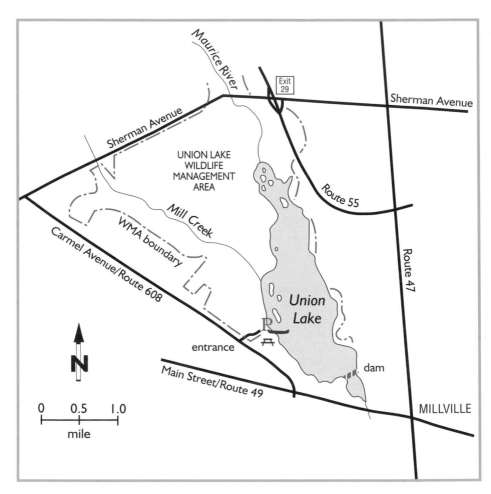

Union Lake

and Elmer Streets in Vineland, displays many of the artifacts uncovered over the years.

While at Union Lake, keep your eyes sharp and you may find a real treasure. If you do find an artifact, take notes on its location as best you can before notifying the historical society. Don't move or remove the item, since archaeologists reconstruct the history of an area based on the exact location of various artifacts. Because this is state-owned property, keeping artifacts is illegal.

Pollution in the form of various chemicals, by-products from a paint production company in North Vineland, once plagued this waterway all the way to Delaware Bay. Dumping stopped in the early 1980s largely due to pressure from surrounding communities and local environmental groups. With the river and lake cleaned up, you'll find not only some of the best fishing in southeastern New Jersey but also some of its cleanest and clearest waters for swimming and paddling. Consider a moonlight paddle here, when the full moon peeks through treetops before spraying a radiant glow across the water.

Bottom sediment consists primarily of tan sand, mud, and some gravel, except near the launch site around the dam, where it is shored up with trucked-in rocks. The average lake depth is 14 feet, with deeper pockets to 30 feet near the dam. Most coves have shallow margins that are only 2 to 4 feet deep—perfect for a refreshing swim. Close to shore you'll find aquatic grasses piercing the water's surface between waterlily pads. In recent years tires and Christmas trees have been used to create artificial habitats. This effort provides key places for juvenile fish to hide from larger predators, thereby helping increase fish populations. Numerous islands, coves, and peninsulas are found on the lake's western and northern areas.

A young paddler in a moment of quiet contemplation at the end of a day.

Of the three islands within 1.0 mile of the put-in off its southwest shore, each has one or two landing sites with small clearings for a picnic lunch and short walking trails to stretch your legs. The largest is Rattlesnake Island, named for the reptile once found in abundance there. Never fear, though—rattlesnakes have not been seen on the island for at least eight years. Largemouth bass, colorful sunfish, catfish, pickerel, and yellow perch are caught by local anglers under the watchful eye of ospreys, which nest along the lake's western shore.

The lake is also stocked with a hybrid fish, a cross between a striped bass and largemouth bass. Ospreys and numerous species of ducks and geese frequent the lake. On a few occasions I've even seen a bald eagle scouting the clear water. Watch carefully and you might spot wood ducks or hooded mergansers, particularly in the coves. At dawn you're likely to see white-tailed deer and raccoons sauntering along the shore. Short cliffs, about 0.75 mile down from the landing, host a few kingfisher nest holes. Look for their cavities about 2 feet above the waterline. If these or any other birds or wildlife exhibit defensive maneuvers when you are near, you should retreat as quietly and unobtrusively as possible, because they may be nesting at the time.

Sandy hiking trails meander along the western and northern lakeshores. Half of the eastern lakefront is residential, but there are some hiking trails along the northeast shore. The trails lead you through an oak and scrub pine forest with lowbush blueberry and sheep laurel dominating the understory. Closer to the water, you'll find red maple, birch, swamp magnolia, cedar, and mountain laurel. In late spring and early summer, dainty, pale pink mountain laurel and white sheep laurel blossoms sprinkle the landscape like pixie dust against a background of dark green cedar and evergreen laurel leaves. Early summer brings the sweet scent of swamp magnolias drifting across the landscape as their large white blossoms unfold.

While outboards are permitted, there is a 10-horsepower limit. Most outboard traffic I have encountered—and there isn't much—has been on the deeper, southeastern end of the lake close to the dam. The best and least crowded paddling is along the lake's western and northern shores, where you can meander around islands and quiet coves.

43

Lake Oswego
Jenkins (Burlington)

MAPS: New Jersey Atlas & Gazetteer, Map 57
USGS Quadrangle, Oswego Lake

AREA: 92 acres

CAMPING: Wading Pines Camping Resort, 85 Godfrey Bridge
Road, Chatsworth, NJ 08019; 888-726-1313. From Lake
Oswego, return to Route 563. Drive south on Route 563 for
1.0 mile. The entrance to the campground is on the right.
Camping is also available at Turtle Run Campground, located
right off Route 542 just 3.2 miles east of Route 563. Turtle
Run Campground, P.O. Box 129, New Gretna, NJ 08224;
609-965-5343.

INFORMATION: Wharton State Forest, 4110 Nesco Road,
Hammonton, NJ 08037; 609-561-0024

HABITAT TYPE: cedar woods

EXPECT TO SEE: waterfowl, ospreys, hawks

TAKE NOTE: electric motorboats only

GETTING THERE

From Route 542, drive north for 6.8 miles on Route 563, turn right onto
Lake Oswego Road, and drive 3.4 miles to the launch site on the right, just
past the guardrailed bridge going over a creek. The old blacktop portion of
the road is bumpy and turns into a sand road near the end. A sign designating
Penn State Forest will be on the right side of the road at the launch site.

Alternately, from Route 532, drive south for 9.6 miles on Route 563 and
turn left onto Lake Oswego Road. Proceed as above.

In the heart of cranberry and blueberry farm country, you will pass one
of Rutgers University's Blueberry and Cranberry Field Research Stations
on the left as you drive to Oswego Lake. Their barn-red buildings with
white trim are somewhat of a landmark in the area. Hawks frequent the
open fields, blue jays screech through the woods, and cardinals dart

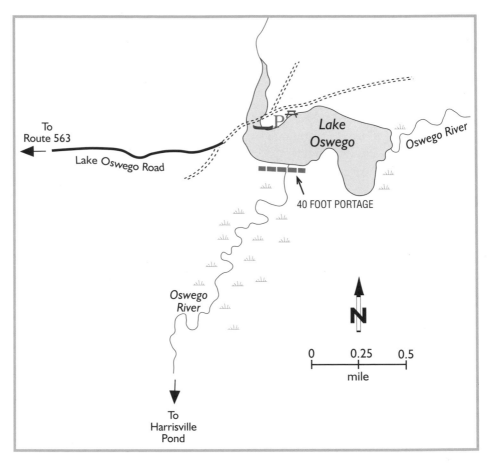

To
Route 563

Lake Oswego Road

Lake
Oswego

Oswego River

P

40 FOOT PORTAGE

Oswego
River

N

0   0.25   0.5
mile

To
Harrisville
Pond

Lake Oswego

through the cedars. I've seen people fish here occasionally, but I've never seen anyone catch anything. There's a small clearing with picnic tables on a point of land east of the launch with a pretty view of the lake.

Cedar, sweetgum, and red maple line the waters within predominantly pine and oak lowland woods studded with American holly, hickory, and elder. Along the bank, look for the tiny, glossy-green leaves of the low-growing cranberry; its green fruit starts to turn red around the middle of August. If you visit in October and November, when the fruits are ripe, be aware that wild cranberries are quite tart. Ocean Spray has facilities near here to make the cranberry juice you buy in the supermarket. The blueberries, however, are sweet and ready to eat. When water levels are high, you can follow the Oswego River upstream from the eastern end of the lake for about 1.0 mile.

Two friends check each other's PFD straps for snugness before heading out on a paddle.

Facing the lake from the launch, look straight across and to the left; you'll see the small dam and a few tiny clearings to the right of it. During paddling season, local outfitters drop off kayak and canoe groups at the launch. They paddle across the lake, portage their boats over the narrow sand dike, and put in at the Oswego River for a three-hour paddle downstream to Harrisville Pond.

Touted as one of the prettiest rivers in the Pine Barrens, the Oswego takes you through Atlantic white cedar swamps, lowland forests, and freshwater marshes. If you want to combine biking and paddling, this is ideal. Lock your bike to a tree at the Harrisville landing, then drive back to Oswego Lake. Paddle around the lake for a while and portage over the small sand dike to put in on the river.

When you arrive at Harrisville Pond, paddle to the landing beach and picnic area at the southern end on the right. The bike ride back to Oswego is an easy 5.0 miles—the land is fairly flat. Since this is a prime biking location, an official bike lane has been designated along Route 679 for safer travel. More roads in the area are slated for similar lanes in the near future.

44

Harrisville Pond
Harrisville (Burlington)

MAPS: New Jersey Atlas & Gazetteer, Map 65
   USGS Quadrangle, Jenkins

AREA: 40 acres

CAMPING: Wading Pines Camping Resort, 85 Godfrey Bridge
   Road, Chatsworth, NJ 08019; 888-726-1313. From
   Harrisville Pond, drive west on Route 679. At the junction
   with Route 563, turn right and drive 1.8 miles to the
   campground entrance on the left.

INFORMATION: Wharton State Forest, 4110 Nesco Road,
   Hammonton, NJ 08037; 609-561-0024

HABITAT TYPE: cedar woods and cedar bogs

EXPECT TO SEE: turtles, waterfowl, bog magnolia

TAKE NOTE: cedar stumps

GETTING THERE

From Route 542, drive north for 5.4 miles on Route 563. Turn right (east)
onto Route 679, and drive 1.4 miles to the launch site and picnic area on the
left. Launch anywhere along the small beach. Parking is informal.

Wild blueberry bushes peek out among the cedar and pine dominating
the shoreline of Harrisville Pond. Mountain and sheep laurel blossoms
bring delicate touches of pink and white to the landscape in early summer, along with the white flowers of the lightly scented bog magnolia.
In midsummer the aroma of sweet pepperbush fills the air as cranberries
begin to grow on its moist shores. Old cedar stumps in the large cove
on the northwest end of the pond are perfect basking spots for turtles.
If you feel energetic, you can paddle to its northeast corner, where the
Oswego River enters, then paddle upstream for about a mile. The first
large cove on the right (east) as you paddle north becomes carpeted
with yellow and white pond lilies in late summer.

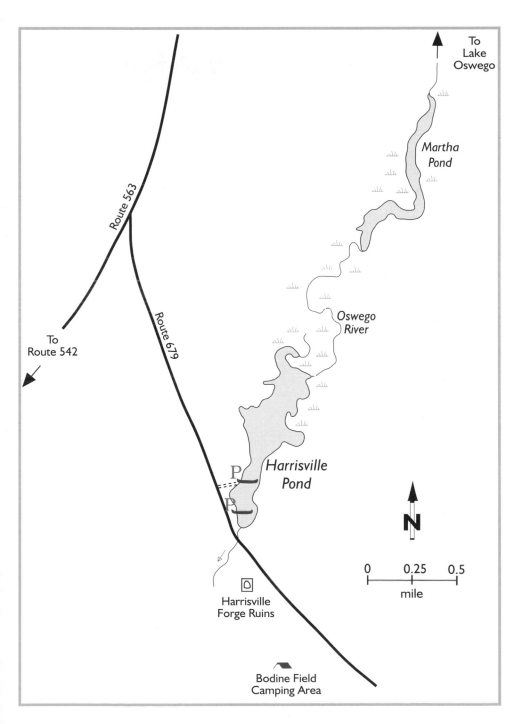

To
Lake
Oswego

Martha
Pond

Route 563

Oswego
River

To
Route 542

Route 679

Harrisville
Pond

P

P

N

0   0.25   0.5

mile

Harrisville
Forge Ruins

Bodine Field
Camping Area

Harrisville Pond

Picking blueberries for a tasty snack.

This is a good opportunity to combine biking and hiking in the same outing by starting your trip on Lake Oswego. See the details under Trip 43.

45

Wilson Lake
Clayton (Gloucester)

Maps: New Jersey Atlas & Gazetteer, Map 62
   USGS Quadrangle, Pitman East
Area: 58 acres
Information: Gloucester County Parks and Recreation,
   6 Blackwood Barnsboro Road, Sewell, NJ 08080; 856-881-0845
Habitat Type: woods and swamp
Expect to See: waterfowl, turtles, hawks
Take Note: electric outboards only

Getting There

From Route 610 (Clayton Road) on the southeast side of Clayton, drive 0.4 mile north on Route 655 (Fries Mill Road) to the park entrance on the right. Follow the signs to the boat launch. Portable toilets are located at the boat launch parking lot.

From Route 322, drive south for 2.5 miles on Route 655 to the park entrance on the left. The nature center at Scotland Run Park sponsors nature lessons, monthly bird walks, and a kid's nature center, which meets once a month.

Scotland Run Park on the southeast side of Clayton contains 900 acres of natural woodlands, hiking trails, and Wilson Lake. A small public beach with picnic tables, a playground, and restrooms occupies 300 feet of shoreline near the dam on the southwest end. Next to the concrete boat ramp, a fishing pier juts about 25 feet into the lake. Only electric motors are allowed, which makes for a quiet paddle. The majority of anglers cast their lines into the deeper waters near the dam for pickerel and smallmouth bass.

A narrow hiking trail starts at the boat ramp along the north lakeshore and continues for 0.5 mile. The longer trail lies along the southern lakeshore and is accessible by foot or by landing on a small

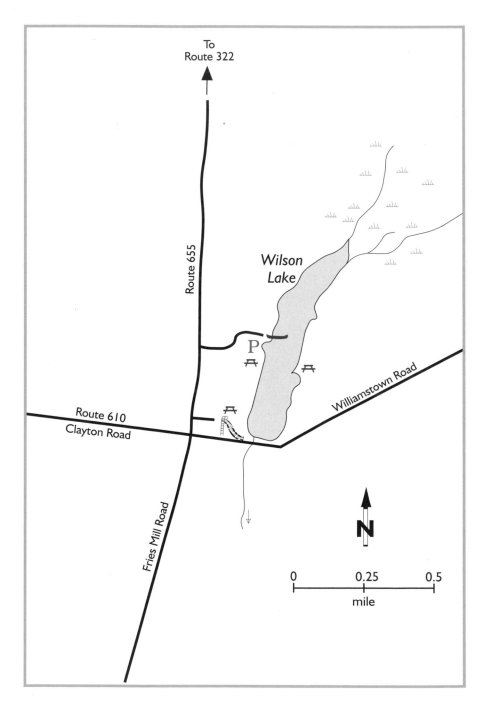

Wilson Lake

One of the many coves to explore on Wilson Lake.

beach at 0.25 mile north of the dam. A few picnic tables are nestled in the nearby woods.

Most of the waters are shallow, averaging 4 feet, with deeper waters in the channel closer to the southern shore. Oak, pine, maple, and beech comprise the upland woods, with cedar and red maple along the water's edge. Where aquatic vegetation approaches the surface, juvenile fish and a few species of turtles can be observed darting in and out of their protective environment.

On the northern end of the lake, where more swamplike conditions exist, cedar, magnolia, sweetgum, pickerelweed, and other water-loving flora dominate the landscape. Boglike coves and stump-strewn inlets create a perfect habitat for birds, turtles, deer, and raccoons. An abundant hawk population almost guarantees you'll see one while paddling—most likely the broad-winged hawk.

46

Lake Lenape
Mays Landing (Atlantic)

MAPS: New Jersey Atlas & Gazetteer, Map 70
  USGS Quadrangle, Mays Landing

AREA: 350 acres

CAMPING: Pleasant Valley Campground is located 1.0 mile south
  of Mays Landing between Mileposts 17 and 18 on Route 50
  and South River Road. Pleasant Valley Campground, Box 73,
  Estell Manor, NJ 08319; 609-625-1238.

INFORMATION: Lake Lenape Park Recreation Center, 753 Park
  Road and 13th Street, P.O. Box 57, Mays Landing, NJ 08330;
  609-625-2021 or 800-626-7612

HABITAT TYPE: woods with some open areas; cedar swamp

EXPECT TO SEE: waterfowl, hawks, turtles, pickerelweed

TAKE NOTE: motorboats are limited to 10 HP

GETTING THERE

From Route 322 (Black Horse Pike), drive south for 1.8 miles on Route 50.
Turn right onto Main Street (Route 559) and drive 0.3 mile to the T. Turn
left onto Mill Street (Route 559) for 0.1 mile, and then turn right onto Old
Harding Highway (also Route 559) for 0.2 mile to the park entrance on the
right. A concrete boat ramp is on the right just before the recreation center.
A small fee is charged during summer to enter the park.

On its way to the Atlantic Ocean, the scenic Great Egg Harbor River
was dammed to create Lake Lenape, most of which lies within the con-
fines of Lake Lenape Park. Private property and the park's recreational
facilities rim the southern end of the lake, but escape to wilder waters is
an easy paddle away. The 1,900-acre park protects major portions of the
Great Egg Harbor River, a nationally designated Wild and Scenic River.
Campsites are available within the park, but they are not lakeside.

Starting from the launch at Lake Lenape's southern tip, paddle
northwest toward the headwaters. Along the way, sightsee around the

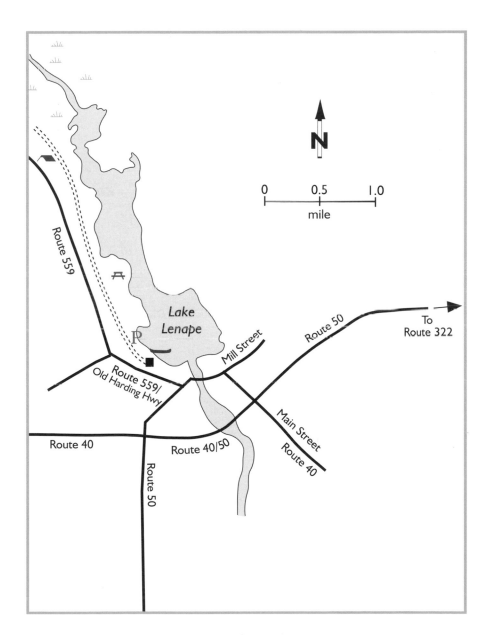

Lake Lenape

Lake Lenape along the Great Egg Harbor River, a nationally designated Wild and Scenic River.

many coves and explore deep inlets. Cedar lines the shores in front of mixed oak-pine forests. Blueberry, sheep laurel, and mulberry bushes fill the understory, while stands of *Phragmites* and cattails grow in open shallows. After passing through the narrower central portion, the lake opens wide and beautiful. In the northwest corner, where the Great Egg Harbor River enters the lake, you can paddle upstream for quite a few miles depending on the water level.

If you have children under twelve, visit nearby Storybook Land, where kids can play in a village built around their favorite stories and classic nursery rhymes. Drive 7.4 miles east on Route 322 from Route 50 to the entrance on the right. Storybook Land, 6415 Route 322, Cardiff, NJ 08234; 609-646-0103.

～ 47 ～

Lake Absegami
New Gretna (Burlington)

MAPS: New Jersey Atlas & Gazetteer, Map 65
 USGS Quadrangle, New Gretna
AREA: 63 acres
CAMPING AND INFORMATION: Bass River State Forest, 762 Stage
 Road, P.O. Box 118, New Gretna, NJ 08224; 609-296-1114
HABITAT TYPE: cedar woods; bogs
EXPECT TO SEE: waterfowl, turtles

GETTING THERE

From Southbound Garden State Parkway: Take Exit 52 immediately after the tollbooth. Turn right onto East Greenbush Road (Route 654) at the end of the ramp and drive 1.1 miles to the T (Stage Road, but there's no sign). Turn right and drive 0.9 mile to the entrance of Bass River State Park, on the left. After passing the booth (a fee is charged in summer), drive straight ahead to the sand boat launch road on the left. Some parking is available at the launch site. A larger parking lot is located at the entrance to the boat launch road.

From Northbound Garden State Parkway: Take Exit 50 (Route 9). The ramp will cross back over the parkway and place you on Route 9 north. Drive 1.9 miles, turn left onto East Greenbush Road, and drive 0.8 mile to the T. Continue as above.

Lake Absegami lies in the northwest corner of the Bass River State Forest at the southern end of Burlington County. The 63-acre body of water offers cedar swamps, bogs, and pine and mixed oak forests surrounding the tea-colored waters typical of the Pine Barrens. Large coves will provide hours of exploring as you discover something new around each bend. Warblers, blue jays, cardinals, kingbirds, eastern pewees, and other songbirds add to the nature experience. While you're there, take advantage of camping in a tent, a lean-to, or a trailer within the pine-scented woodlands. The park also rents rustic cabins, a

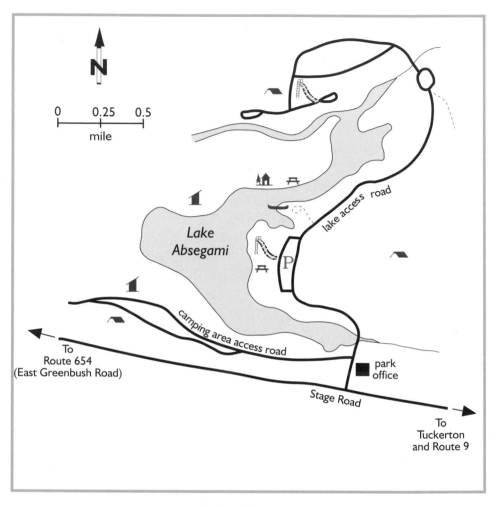

Lake Absegami

few of which are lakeside. Schedule your trip around a full-moon cycle to enjoy a pleasant moonlight paddle before retiring. Playgrounds are located at the swimming beach and within the camping area.

The cedar-lined shore provides enjoyable lakeside camping.

48

Corbin City Impoundments
Tuckahoe (Atlantic)

MAPS: New Jersey Atlas & Gazetteer, Map 70
USGS Quadrangle, Marmora

AREA: Impoundment 1, 104 acres
Impoundment 2, 243 acres
Impoundment 3, 284 acres

CAMPING: Holiday Haven Campground is located 0.5 mile south
on Route 50 from the Gibson's Creek Road exit from the
compounds. Holiday Haven Campground, 230 Route 50,
Woodbine, NJ, 08270; 609-476-2963. The Scenic Riverview
Campground is also nearby, in Tuckahoe. Take Route 50
south to Route 49 west and drive 2.5 miles; the entrance is on
the right. Scenic River Campground, 465 Route 49, P.O. Box
184, Tuckahoe, NJ 08250; 609-628-4566.

INFORMATION: New Jersey Division of Fish and Wildlife,
Southern Region (Winslow WMA), 229 Blue Anchor Road,
Sicklerville, NJ 08081; 856-629-0090

HABITAT TYPE: marsh

EXPECT TO SEE: waterfowl, wading birds, songbirds,
kingfishers, ospreys

TAKE NOTE: electric outboards only

GETTING THERE

Parking and launching are informal at best throughout the wildlife management area. A few openings here and there through the narrow border of
shrubs and trees rimming the impoundments provide access to the waters and
enough widening in the road for a few cars to parallel park. Hug the edge
when you park so as not to block other cars. Below are directions to some of
the better launch spots. You're likely to find an angler or two pulled over to
the side near the floodgate for each impoundment.

From Route 50 in Corbin City at its junction with Route 611 (Aetna
Road), drive west for 0.7 mile on Route 50 and turn right onto Griscom Mill
Road. A sign for the wildlife management area is on Route 50, but it is placed
parallel to the road and thus hard to see. After turning onto Griscom Mill

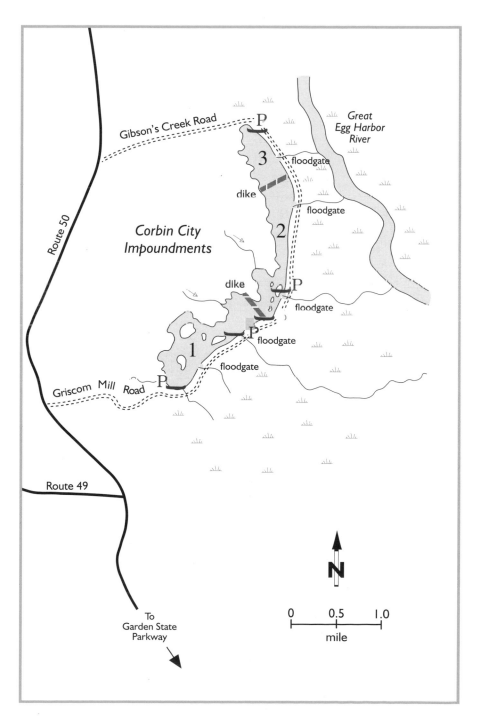

Corbin City Impoundments

Road, drive 0.4 mile to where the blacktop ends and a sand road begins. Continue for another 1.6 miles, following the main sand road to the southern end of the south impoundment. There is room to park your car here and launch from the sandy embankment. For the next launch to the south impoundment, drive another 0.5 mile to a small clearing between the shrubs on the left.

For access to the middle impoundment, continue for another 0.3 mile to the right bend in the road, where you can launch into the southern end of the middle impoundment. Drive another 0.4 mile to another launch area—my favorite, because kingfishers are easy to spot here. Continue for another 1.3 miles for access to the north impoundment. From this point, continue driving on the main sand road, now called Gibson's Creek Road, for 2.2 miles to the junction of Route 50. You will be 3.5 miles farther north on Route 50 from where you started.

To get to Route 50 from the Garden State Parkway, take Exit 29 and turn west onto Route 623 (Roosevelt Boulevard). Drive 0.8 mile, following a curve to the left onto Route 631 (Tuckahoe Road). Drive for 4.9 miles to its junction with Route 50. Turn right (west) onto Route 50 and continue as above.

Part of the excitement is not knowing what you are going to find around the next bend.

We share the waters with these elegant year-round residents.

Get ready for great birding and remote, peaceful paddling. Impoundments, similar to shallow reservoirs, are large dammed areas creating basins to collect and confine waters. Three large impoundments, ranging from 104 to 284 acres, lie within the Lester G. MacNamara Wildlife Management Area not far from the Great Egg Harbor River. All offer the spectacular scenery typical of lands bordering brackish marshes, where lowland woods stand behind the water-loving plants that frame creeks and ponds. Here you will find a mix of flora and fauna from freshwater and saltwater environments: hawks, muskrats, deer, foxes, shorebirds, ospreys, egrets, kingfishers, warblers, and numerous species of songbirds.

While all three impoundments offer the nature lover spectacular opportunities, the southern impoundments offer a more adventurous trip, as you wind your way around numerous islands and into large coves. Kingfishers are most abundant in the second impoundment, where slightly steeper banks provide a better nesting habitat. Swans add a calm elegance, their snowy bodies contrasting against dark waters. Egrets and herons stalk the shallows everywhere, their long necks stretched out, searching for small fish swimming just beneath the surface. Don't forget your camera and lots of film for this trip. Electric outboards are permitted on the waters.

49

Stewart Lake
Woodbury (Gloucester)

MAPS: New Jersey Atlas & Gazetteer, Map 54
   USGS Quadrangle, Woodbury
AREA: 45 acres
HABITAT TYPE: open woods; development
EXPECT TO SEE: waterfowl, turtles, pond lilies, raccoons
TAKE NOTE: electric outboards only; no camping within a 30-
   minute drive

GETTING THERE

From Route 534 (Good Intent Road), drive west for 1.5 miles on Route 506 (Cooper Street). Slow down after you pass under the turnpike bridge, because the entrance to the boat launch on the right comes up fast. Turn right into the boat launch area then park courteously (parking is limited).

There's an alternate launch location from the park's recreational site, where a large lakeside picnic grove and playground are provided. From Route 534 (Good Intent Road), drive west for 2.3 miles on Route 506, turn right (north) onto Evergreen Street, and drive 1.2 miles, turning right onto Red Bank Avenue. Then drive 0.1 mile to the park's entrance on the right. Turn into the park, drive past the building on the right, then head over to the right side of the rear parking lot, where you will see a sign for the boat launch at the head of a dirt road.

Stewart Lake's 45 acres are surrounded entirely by a municipal park. In some areas the woods thin, leaving only a modest screen between you and civilization; elsewhere they provide a thick blanket of insulation. Upland woods of maple, hickory, sassafras, tulip, ash, and pine delight you with splashes of red, orange, and yellow in fall and cool greens in summer. There's abundant wildlife to be found and attractive scenery that's easy on the eyes. Raccoons, possums, and skunks are more likely to be spotted on the thickly wooded northeast end near the boat

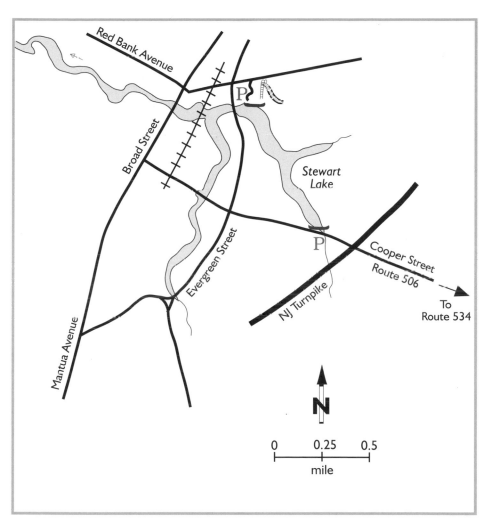

Stewart Lake

Heavily wooded parklands grace the northern end of the lake near the boat ramp.

launch, while turtles and frogs are more prevalent in shallow areas on the eastern banks. Only electric outboards are permitted, so it will be quiet on the water. Recreational facilities are centrally located on the north side of this horseshoe-shaped lake, but only the tree-studded picnic area is lakeside.

~ 50 ~

Parvin Lake and Thundergust Lake
Centerton (Salem)

MAPS: New Jersey Atlas & Gazetteer, Map 62
    USGS Quadrangle, Elmer

AREA: Parvin Lake, 95 acres
    Thundergust Lake, 14 acres

CAMPING AND INFORMATION: Parvin State Park, 701 Almond
    Road, Pittsgrove, NJ 08318; 609-358-8616

HABITAT TYPE: cedar and oak woods; bogs

EXPECT TO SEE: waterfowl, turtles, hawks

TAKE NOTE: electric outboards only

GETTING THERE

From Route 77, drive east for 6.0 miles on Route 540 to the entrance and park office on the right. Signs are posted prominently along Route 540. If you do not stop at the park office, continue for another 0.3 mile, turn right onto Parvin Mill Road, and drive 0.15 mile to the launch site on the right.

More than 1,100 acres of Parvin State Park are yours to enjoy for paddling, camping, fishing, and hiking. Mountain laurel and dogwood lend a delicate scent to the air in late spring, when their blossoms open wide to splash the landscape with color. Seventeen miles of hiking trails lead you through sweetly scented Atlantic white cedar swamps, lowland and upland hardwood forests, and mixed oak-pine forests, typical of the Pine Barrens. The park is home to the state-threatened barred owl and the endangered swamp pink, whose pink blossoms in late spring stand atop 2-foot stalks. When you visit the swamp, search for the carnivorous pitcher plant, which thrives in this moist, acidic environment. Bog and painted turtles are common in the swamps and around the lakes. Parvin State Park is noted as a hot spot for the spring migration of neotropical songbirds.

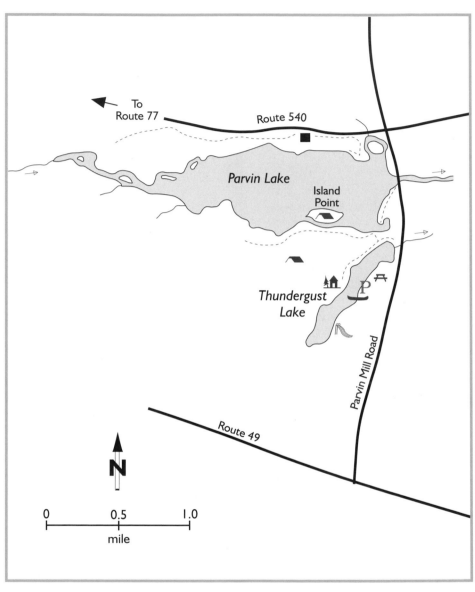

To
Route 77

Route 540

Parvin Lake

Island
Point

Thundergust
Lake

P

Parvin Mill Road

Route 49

N

0   0.5   1.0
mile

Parvin Lake and Thundergust Lake

Looking down Parvin Lake from the boat launch facility.

Two lakes within the park, 95-acre Parvin Lake and 14-acre Thundergust Lake, give you plenty of water in which to paddle. In addition to tent sites, the park offers one group campsite on an island and lakeside cabins along the shore at Thundergust Lake. July and August bring crowds, so make camping reservations well in advance, particularly if you want one of the lakeside cabins.

Appendix: Resources

Map Sources

Ramsey Outdoor Stores
1039 Route 46 West
Ledgewood, NJ 07852
973-584-7799

Around the World in Maps
1305 New York Avenue
Manasquan, NJ 08736
732-223-5899

To obtain free map indexes and catalogs or to order topographic maps:
United States Geological Survey Information Services
P.O. Box 25286
Denver, CO 80225
888-275-8747 or 303-202-4700

For topographic maps with detailed hiking trails:
New York–New Jersey Trail Conference (NYNJTC)
232 Madison Avenue, No. 802
New York, NY 10016
Office hours: M–F 11 A.M.–5:30 P.M.
212-685-9699

Paddling Equipment and Technique

Gullion, Laurie. *The Canoeing and Kayaking Instruction Manual.* Springfield, VA: American Canoe Association, 1993.

Knapp, Andy. *The Optimum Kayak: How to Choose, Maintain, Repair, and Customize the Right Boat for You.* Camden, ME: Ragged Mountain Press, 2000.

Rowe, Ray. *Teach Yourself Canoeing: A Practical Introduction to Canoeing and Kayaking.* Lincolnwood, IL: NTC Publishing Group, 1993.

Protecting the Environment

Hampton, Bruce, and David Cole. *Soft Paths.* Mechanicsburg, PA: Stackpole Books, 1995.

McGiveny, Annette. *Leave No Trace: A Practical Guide to the New Wilderness Ethic.* Branson, MO: Mountaineers Books, 1998.

Meyer, Kathleen. *How to Shit in the Woods.* Berkeley, CA: Ten Speed Press, 1994.

Camping/Campgrounds

Daniel, Linda. *Kayak Cookery*. Guilford, CT: Globe Pequot Press, 1986. (I hope none of my friends discovers that I know about this book; they may expect gourmet meals.)

Getchell, Annie. *The Essential Outdoor Gear Manual*. Camden, ME: Ragged Mountain Press, 1995.

Harrison, David. *Kayak Camping*. New York: Hearst Books, 1995.

Kuhne, Cecil. Kayak Touring and Camping. Mechanicsburg, PA: Stackpole Books, 1999.

Woodall Publishing. *The Complete Guide to Campgrounds, RV Parks, Service Centers and Attractions: Mid-Atlantic Camping Guide*. Lake Forest, IL: Woodall Publishing Corp., 2000.

Taking the Kids Along

Harrison, David, and Judy Harrison. *Canoe Tripping with Children*. Guilford, CT: Globe Pequot Press, 1990.

Woodson, Roger, and Kimberley Woodson. *The Parent's Guide to Camping with Children*. Cincinnati: Betterway Books, 1995.

Useful Addresses and Phone Numbers

Appalachian Mountain Club
5 Joy Street
Boston, MA 02108
617-523-0636; www.outdoors.org
New York–North Jersey Chapter
212-986-1430

Appalachian Mountain Club
Mohican Outdoor Center
50 Camp Road
Blairstown, NJ 07825-9655
908-362-5670

Green Acres Program
501 East State Street
Station Plaza Building 5, Ground Floor
Trenton, NJ 08609-1101
609-984-0500

New Jersey Audubon Society Headquarters
9 Hardscrabble Road
P.O. Box 126

Bernardsville, NJ 07924
908-204-8998
The Nature Conservancy
New Jersey Field Office
Elizabeth D. Kay Environmental Center
200 Pottersville Road
Chester, NJ 07930
908-879-7262

The Sierra Club
57 Mountain Avenue
Princeton, NJ 08540
609-924-3141

New Jersey Division of Fish and Wildlife
P.O. Box 400
Trenton, NJ 08625
609-292-2965

New Jersey Recreation and Parks Association
4 Griggstown Causeway
Princeton, NJ 08540
908-281-9212

New Jersey Division of Parks and Forestry
501 East State Street, P.O. Box 404
Trenton, NJ 08625
800-843-6420

For general information about wildlife management areas:
Pequest Trout Hatchery and Natural Resource Education Center
605 Pequest Road
Oxford, NJ 07863
908-637-4125

Alphabetical Listing of Lakes, Ponds, and Reservoirs

Assunpink Lake 75

Atsion Lake 116

Batsto Lake 110

Bridge to Nowhere 132

Colliers Mill Lake 98

Columbia Lake 40

Cooper River Park Lake 127

Corbin City Impoundments 164

Cranberry Lake 53

Delaware and Raritan Canal 58

East Creek Pond 138

Farrington Lake 94

Forge Pond 78

Gardner's Pond 6

Great Bay and the Edwin B. Forsythe
  National Wildlife Refuge 141

Green Turtle Pond 23

Hackensack Meadows 10

Harrisville Pond 152

Lake Absegami 161

Lake Aeroflex 6

Lake Carasaljo 64

Lake Hopatcong 45

Lake Lenape 158

Lake Mercer 90

Lake Musconetcong 45

Lake Nummy 138

Lake Oswego 149

Lake Shenandoah 64

Lake Success 98

Lake Surprise 62

Lake Topanemus 92

Manahawkin Impoundment 132

Manasquan Reservoir 69

Mannington Meadows 120

Merrill Creek Reservoir 42

Monksville Reservoir 20

Newton Lake 127

Oxford Furnace Lake 38

Parvin Lake 171

Paulins Kill Lake 31

Pompton Lake 14

Prospertown Lake 72

Rising Sun Lake 75

Round Valley Reservoir 83

Sawmill Lake 2

Shadow Lake 80

Shaw's Mill Pond 130

Shepherd Lake 17

Silver Lake 50

Spruce Run Reservoir 87

Stafford Forge Ponds 124

Steeny Kill Lake 2

Stewart Lake 168

Stone Tavern Lake 75

Swartswood Lake 31

Thundergust Lake 171

Turn Mill Lake 98

Twin Lakes 6

Union Lake 145

Wawayanda Lake 26

Weequahic Lake 105

White's Lake 36

Whites Pond 6

Whitesbog Ponds 102

Wilson Lake 155

Leave No Trace

The Appalachian Mountain Club is a national educational partner of Leave No Trace, Inc., a nonprofit organization dedicated to promoting and inspiring responsible outdoor recreation through education, research, and partnerships. The Leave No Trace Program seeks to develop wildland ethics—ways in which people think and act in the outdoors to minimize their impacts on the areas they visit and to protect our natural resources for future enjoyment. Leave No Trace unites four federal land management agencies—the U.S. Forest Service, National Park Service, Bureau of Land Management, and U.S. Fish and Wildlife Service—with manufacturers, outdoor retailers, user groups, educators, organizations like the AMC and the National Outdoor Leadership School (NOLS), and individuals.

The Leave No Trace ethic is guided by these seven principles:

- Plan ahead and prepare.
- Travel and camp on durable surfaces.
- Dispose of waste properly.
- Leave what you find.
- Minimize campfire impacts.
- Respect wildlife.
- Be considerate of other visitors.

The AMC has joined NOLS—a recognized leader in wilderness education and a founding partner of Leave No Trace—as the sole national providers of the Leave No Trace Master Educator course through 2004. The AMC offers this five-day course, designed especially for outdoor professionals and land managers, as well as the shorter two-day Leave No Trace Trainer course at locations throughout the Northeast.

For Leave No Trace information and materials, contact:
Leave No Trace, Inc.
P.O. Box 997
Boulder, CO 80306
800-332-4100
www.LNT.org

About the Author

KATHY KENLEY is a marine biologist with additional degrees in geology and creative writing. She started kayaking in 1966, and since then has explored and paddled lakes, ponds, rivers, and coastal marshes along the East Coast and as far away as Thailand and Fiji. She has competed on the national level in many kayak races, and occasionally leads guided tours for a local outfitter within the Pine Barrens of southern New Jersey. Her current focus is to help introduce older men and women to the world of paddling.

Kenley, an avid scuba diver and snorkeler, owned and operated her own charter dive boat for more than ten years and holds a U.S. Coast Guard captain's license. Her numerous eclectic interests range from paleontology to art and anthropology. She is committed to protecting the environment, participating in waterway cleanups, and carrying a trash bag in her boat to pick up discarded refuse.

About the AMC

Since 1876, the Appalachian Mountain Club has helped people experience the majesty and solitude of the Northeast outdoors. We offer outdoor skills workshops, guided trips, and lodging options for all levels of outdoor adventuring.
Our conservation programs include trail maintenance, air and water quality research, and advocacy work to preserve the special outdoor places we love and enjoy for future generations.

Join the Adventure!

Take a hike, ride a bike, paddle a canoe. We believe that people who enjoy breathing fresh air, climbing mountains, splashing in streams, and walking on trails have more fun and take better care of the outdoors. Join the fun today. Call 617-523-0636 for membership information.

Outdoor Adventures

From beginner backpacking to advanced backcountry skiing, we teach outdoor skills workshops to suit your interest and experience. If you prefer the company of others and skilled leaders, we also offer guided hiking and paddling trips. Our five outdoor education centers guarantee year-round adventures.

Huts, Lodges, and Visitor Centers

With accommodations throughout the Northeast, you don't have to travel to the ends of the earth to see nature's beauty and experience unique wilderness lodging. Accessible by car or on foot, our lodges and huts are perfect for families, couples, groups, and individuals.

Books and Maps

We can lead you to the best hiking, biking, skiing, and paddling destinations from Maine to North Carolina. With more than fifty books and maps published, we're your definitive resource for discovering wonderful outdoor places. For ordering information call 800-262-4455.

Check us out online at www.outdoors.org, where there's lots going on.

Appalachian Mountain Club
5 Joy Street
Boston, MA 02108
617-523-0636